THE STAGE AND SOC~~IAL~~
STRUGGLE IN EARLY~~ MODERN~~
ENGL~~AND~~

The Stage and Social Struggle in Early Modern England is a ground-breaking study of theater's controversial and contradictory place in the social transformations of the Tudor and Stuart period.

In language both lucid and theoretically sophisticated, Jean Howard examines the gap between the overheated attacks on the stage and the theater's actual role in class, gender, and sexual conflict. She analyses canonized plays by Shakespeare and Jonson as well as little-studied dramas such as *The Whore of Babylon* and *The Wise Woman of Hogsdon*. In doing so Howard looks at how the stage absorbed and transformed antitheatrical polemic as part of its own participation in the social struggles to which the antitheatricalists were responding.

An exciting challenging and eminently readable work, *The Stage and Social Struggle in Early Modern England* is an important addition to early modern cultural studies.

Jean E. Howard teaches Renaissance Literature and Critical Theory at Columbia University. She is co-editor, with Marion O'Connor, of *Shakespeare Reproduced: The Text in History and Ideology,* and is US Associate Editor of the journal *Textual Practice,* both published by Routledge. She is also the author of *Shakespeare's Art of Orchestration: Stage Technique and Audience Response.*

THE STAGE AND SOCIAL STRUGGLE IN EARLY MODERN ENGLAND

Jean E. Howard

London and New York

First published 1994
by Routledge
11 New Fetter Lane, London EC4P 4EE

Simultaneously published in the USA and Canada
by Routledge
29 West 35th Street, New York, NY 10001

Phototypeset in Palatino by Intype, London

Printed and bound in Great Britain by
Clays Ltd, St Ives PLC

Printed on acid free paper

British Library Cataloguing in Publication Data

A catalogue record for this book is available from the British Library

Library of Congress Cataloging in Publication Data

Applied for

ISBN 0–415–04258–5 (hbk)
ISBN 0–415–09553–0 (pbk)

For Caleb, Child of Light

CONTENTS

ACKNOWLEDGMENTS

Life makes finishing books hard, at least for me. That this one sees the light is largely due to the emotional and intellectual sustenance provided by friends and by my family – all of it. I especially want to thank Felicity Nussbaum, Phyllis Rackin, Ann Douglas, and David Kastan for being extraordinary colleagues; Kate McCluskie and Walter Cohen for intellectual companionship of the highest order; and the graduate students at Columbia for reminding me daily why teaching is the best possible job. The Folger Library and the colleagues connected with it – especially Gail Paster, Lena Orlin, and Barbara Mowat – have been indispensable to this project and to my sanity. Betsy and Charlie Wallace, Carolyn Carter, and Michael McTighe have been necessary friends, it seems, for forever.

Portions of this book were published in earlier drafts in *Shakespeare Quarterly*, *Renaissance Drama* and *Shakespeare Reproduced*, the collection of essays I edited with my dear friend, Marion O'Connor. I am grateful for permission to reproduce revised versions of those essays here. I owe special thanks to Allison Outland and Ruth Samson Luborsky for helping me find the woodcut now on the cover of this book. Professor Luborsky's *A Guide to English Illustrated Books 1536–1603* is forthcoming from Scholar Press. Finally I wish to thank Janice Price and Talia Rodgers for superb editorial counsel and support. Ralph and Ellie, Barb and Dan, Aaron, Rebecca, Katie, Caleb, and Jim have provided the sustaining context.

RENAISSANCE THEATER AND THE REPRESENTATION OF THEATRICAL PRACTICE

A brief for political criticism

In 1603 Edward Jorden, a doctor, published a tract entitled *A Briefe Discourse of a Disease called the Suffocation of the Mother*. He dedicated it to the President and Fellows of the College of Physicians in London. The purpose of the tract was to dispel various myths surrounding the disease known as "the mother" and to place its treatment on a scientific footing. Consequently, the body of the tract is devoted to discussing the womb, why it becomes stopped with superfluous matter, and how it can be regulated. Those who suffer from the mother, particularly young girls and widows, are enjoined to avoid sweet savors, pleasant meats, too much rest, and mental perturbation, especially lovesick thoughts. Helpfully, Jorden urges that those who *do* suffer from lovesickness should either be induced to hate their object of affection or to enjoy their desires (Jorden 1603: G4).

Of particular importance and interest, however, is the way Jorden frames the tract. It opens with an attack on those who do not approach the mother properly – i.e., as a disease proceeding from natural causes – but improperly – i.e., as a manifestation of demonic possession. In particular, he ridicules Papists who pull out their wooden daggers to exorcize a maid or woman who is suffering from a natural disorder that can easily be cured by fasting and prayer (Jorden 1603: A3). He goes on, moreover, to accuse priests of actually suborning people to "counterfait strange motions and behaviours" so that the priests can have the glory of rescuing them by making the sign of the cross and muttering "powerlesse spelles" (Jorden 1603: A3). This, of course, sounds familiar to those who have read Stephen Greenblatt's work on the Anglican attacks on exorcism in the period (1988: 94–128). Those who approach the mother as evidence of demonic possession are not only, except in rare cases, presented as wrong; they are also presented as tricksters who stage theatrical shows to gain power illegitimately. This is opposed to the solid, "real" knowledge of the medical man who works substantively, not theatrically.

But ends of narratives have ways of forgetting their beginnings. After Jorden has patiently given his medical account of the mother and how to cure it, he finds himself having to confess that sometimes treatment just doesn't work. Affections and perturbations of the mind affect disease, and these things are not easily mastered. Consequently, he outlines a series of tricks for friends and attendants to use with patients if reasonable treatments fail. These include having a son say to his mother, who believed her symptoms to be caused by the devil, that in her looking glass he had seen a "great" devil drive out three other devils, leaving her free from possession (G4); or putting nails, feathers, and other objects in a woman's close-stool to make her believe she had rid herself of the cause of her distress in the process of defecating (G4-G4^v). He goes on to list a range of superstitious remedies (love potions, charms, exorcisms, amulets, incense, holy water, offerings to saints, pissing through a wedding ring, etc.) which may be used in extreme cases, not because they have efficacy in themselves, but because people believe in them. As he says: "we may politikely confirme them in their fantasies, that wee may the better fasten some cure upon them" (Jorden 1603: G4^v). Jorden has not assented to the view that the mother and other diseases are caused by demonic possession, but he has undermined his claim that symptoms result solely from physical causes such as a surfeit of roast beef, and he has dangerously blurred the line between himself, the designer of these "tricks," and the theatrical, cross-waving Papists.

Ostensibly, what separates Jorden from the Papists is his desire to help, and their lust for power, yet Jorden's whole tract is part of a larger movement to take power over men and women's bodies from the hands of cunning women and midwives and village healers and to vest it in the hands of the men of the College of Physicians to whom he dedicated his tract, just as it is part of the larger movement to take control over men and women's souls from the godless Papists and to vest it in the hands of godly Protestants. All may have recourse at times to tricks, disguises, and theatrical deceits, but only some can do so "legitimately," i.e. without being branded as mere powerhungry tricksters.

In this book I am going to examine the political consequences of the way a variety of Renaissance texts, but especially and particularly stage plays, represent those people and groups who engage in theatrical practices. Jorden's representation of the cross-waving Papists staging scenes of false exorcism constitutes one small example of how some behaviors get coded as "merely theatrical" in the sense of deceptive, empty of truth or substance, while other behaviors, such as Jorden's own deceptions of his stubborn patients, which to all appearances seem remarkably like the exorcists' practices, get read and interpreted *differently*, as part of legitimate medical healing. At such moments it is possible to glimpse the power of language, and the power of those who control language, to make crucial political and ideological distinctions between similar phenomena.

By identifying a discourse of theatricality operating in a variety of Renaissance texts and by examining its political functions – its complex and sometimes contradictory role in producing and underwriting various modes of social and moral stratification – I wish to define the ideological work performed by a particular discourse in early modern England. At the same time, in focusing on the theater itself as the site where many of these representations of theatrical behaviors and practices were enacted, I have a second objective, and that is to comment on the unique role of the public theater in ideological production in Renaissance England. This book is as much a study of an institution as of a particular discourse. I wish to investigate which social groups had their interests served through the public theater: to what extent it confirmed traditional distributions of power and to what extent it made space for emergent or marginalized groups. In regard to these questions, nearly all sweeping generalizations are likely to be vulnerable; nonetheless, I will venture some, while trying to remain alert to the contradictions and complexities that make this topic interesting and important, rather than merely an occasion for a mechanical application of a thesis about the rise of the bourgeoisie or the power of patriarchy.

In fact, what most concerns me are the *contradictions* marking not just the theater's representations of theatricality but, in a larger and more general sense, its total role in ideological production. Consideration of these contradictions prompts my third and most abstract concern: how particular, historically specific institutions, of which the Renaissance public theater is but one instance, effect social change in ways that may or may not be consistent across the range of their practices and may or may not be perceptible to those within such institutions or to contemporaneous observers of them. One of the most fascinating aspects of the Renaissance debates about the theater is how variously this institution was interpreted by contemporaries and how differently they described the "lessons" it taught, the social consequences it effected. Later in this book, writing from a position in the present, I will assess some of these early modern narratives about the theater. My purpose will be to show how contemporaries made sense of this troublesome but magnetic institution in their midst, and to delineate where their perceptions diverge from or coincide with my own.

I have in part found it useful to focus on representations of theatricality as a way of talking concretely about the ideological function of the Renaissance public stage because regulating, and controlling access to, theatrical power were crucial political issues in the Renaissance. Many highly theatrical practices – including royal processions, executions, exorcisms, charivaris, chivalric jousts – served as occasions to display, acquire, and exercise power within a fluid social field. While the ensuing bourgeois era would rely more and more heavily upon an expanding print culture to create self-regulating subjects, the Renaissance employed spectacles – including spectacles of exemplary violence, spectacles of monarchical display, and the spectacles of the public stage – as crucial elements of social control and ideological dissemination, a point made by, among others, Francis Barker (1984: esp. 3–41), Michel Foucault (1979: esp. 3–69), Jonathan Goldberg (1983: esp. 28–54), Stephen Greenblatt (1988: esp. 64–5), and Christopher Pye (1990).

But it is important to distinguish one cultural site, and one form of theatrical spectacle, from another. Stage plays, for example, were identical neither in their constitutive elements nor in their social effects to executions or to royal entries. Moreover, the theater was not simply an extension of monarchical power. The stage had to thrive in the marketplace as surely as it was answerable to the royal censor. Its spectacles were commodities which the public paid money to see and over which, consequently, they exercised a certain degree of control. Even at the time of composition, the political and moral import of these stage fictions was very much in dispute. Some commentators, such as Thomas Heywood in his *An Apology for Actors*, asserted that the theater was an ornament to the City of London and that its fictions inculcated moral virtue and respect for authority. As he wrote:

> Playes are writ in this ayme, and carryed with this methode, to teach the subjects obedience to their King, to shew the people the untimely ends of such as have moved tumults, commotions, and insurrections, to present them with the flourishing estate of such as live in obedience, exhorting them to allegeance, dehorting them from all trayterous and fellonious strategems.
>
> (1612: Book III, F3^v)

Others passionately disagreed. In his *A Refutation of the Apology for Actors* J. G. (Green?) retorted that the plays cannot inculcate morality since they are "wholly composed of Fables and Vanities," "lyes and decepts" (1615: F), while the theater itself, rather than an ornament to the City, is "Venus Pallace and Sathans Synagogue" (H2). With perfect certainty he insists that at plays one sees only profane gallants, city dames, country clowns, whores, cutpurses, pickpockets, knaves, and youths, while never laying eyes on ancient citizens, chaste matrons, modest maids, grave Senators, wise magistrates, just judges, or godly preachers (I^v). One wonders, of course, about the status of these categories. How does one tell a "city dame" from a "chaste matron"? Is going to the theater the act that, in the eyes of J. G., *ipso facto* moves one from the second category into the first? Despite their enormous differences, the common ground shared by Heywood and J. G. is, of course, that each assumes that significant power resides in the stage and its spectacles. Theatricality, now institutionalized and commodified, had become an object of cultural contestation. Beneath all the arguments about its morality, I will argue, lurked the urgent question of who would control the implicit power of this institution. Would this power be harnessed to the service of dominant social groups and institutions or appropriated by those perceived as threats to their ascendency? And, of course, what no one at the time could adequately assess was the extent to which the operations of the marketplace would complicate all attempts to control the theater's political investments and effects.

Certainly the theater was a source of anxiety in the period. Formal attacks on and defenses of the stage were numerous and strident, beginning with John Northbrooke's treatise of 1577 and climaxing with William Prynne's gargantuan *Histrio-Mastix* of 1633. In chapter 2 I look at this body of polemical literature, though I do not assume it can be read "straight" as an accurate account of how the theater operated or of the cultural effects it produced. On the other hand, I do not regard this material as simply one more manifestation of an antitheatrical prejudice endemic to western culture.[1] Rather, I read it for traces of the historically specific social struggles and dislocations manifesting themselves as attacks on the theater and on what are described as the theatrical practices of particular social groups. One of the remarkable facts about these tracts is the way that, although in the first instance about a particular social institution, their objects of denigration multiply uncontrollably. Social climbers, rogues and vagabonds, unruly women, Catholic priests – the antitheatrical tracts have damning words for them all. Clearly, the theater became the focus for discharging anxieties about many sorts of social changes or threats to established power. This does not mean that the theater was not disturbing in and of itself, simply that antitheatrical discourse eventually emerged as an all-purpose language of stigmatization and delegitimation, and through it more than the theater or professional actors could be branded as outsiders, criminals, pretenders. I will show that in attacking the stage the antitheatrical tracts provided interested readings of the Elizabethan and Jacobean social order that advanced and/or undermined the claims to power of a *variety* of social groups.

This process was obviously never straightforward, however, either as it occurred through the antitheatrical tracts or especially through stage fictions. This is partly because the axes of domination and subordination in the culture were multiple and not necessarily homologous. Through their representations of theatricality texts variously participated in the construction of race, class, religious, and gender differences and the relations of domination and subordination upheld by those differences,

6

but there is no necessary and inevitable correlation, for example, between a text's gender and class politics.[2] Each has to be examined in its specificity. Moreover, it does not seem to me true that these texts always served established power, whether one defines established power as the monarchy, the aristocracy, the Anglican Church, or the male sex. As I hope to show, the drama enacted ideological contestation as much as it mirrored or reproduced anything that one could call the dominant ideology of a single class, class faction, or sex.

Partly, as Catherine Belsey has argued (1985a: 9–10), that is because dramatic narrative feeds on conflict and the postponement of resolution. Plays for the public stage were not, by and large, overtly homiletic, committed to the straightforward promulgation of dogma. Frequently composed by several hands and cobbling together a variety of discursive and narrative conventions, the drama often accommodated ideologically incompatible elements within a single text. Rather than as signs of aesthetic failure, these incompatibilities can be read as traces of ideological struggle, of differences within the sense-making machinery of culture. Moreover, theater involves more than scripts. It involves a particular scene of production, particular historically specific relations between audience and actor, playwright and theater owner. It will be one of the chief arguments of this book that in the English Renaissance the material practices attendant upon stage production and theatergoing had ideological consequences for the audience that were in some instances at odds with the ideological import of the dramatic fables which that theater disseminated. To show the role of the theater in social change means attending to just such contradictions.

Moreover, as scholars of early modern drama have increasingly become aware, "Shakespeare" is not synonymous with Renaissance drama. He did not work extensively in some of the most vital dramatic genres of his time, such as city comedy, and his work encodes the ideologies of the aristocracy more centrally than do, for example, the plays of Dekker or Heywood. This book began as a study of Shakespeare; but it ended up as a consideration of plays by a number of other dramatists, as well, precisely because Shakespeare alone – despite the enormous reputation he has acquired in subsequent centuries – offers material for a very partial picture of Renaissance theater. In enlarging my scope beyond Shakespeare, however, I have not attempted to give anything like a history of the stage in this period. I pay almost no attention, for example, to the boy companies; do not try to trace the evolution of a single dramatic genre, despite a distinct partiality for histories and for comedy in all its forms; and do not attempt in any systematic way to map changes in the theater's complex relations to the monarch and to state power in the decades between 1576 and 1642. Instead, I focus on clusters of texts in which the representation of the theater or of theatricality is a central issue and from this focus examine the ideological work performed by these texts in the venues in which they were first produced. Because my intent is to delineate what is distinctive about the theater's role in ideological production in the period, I consider not only how dramatic spectacles and scripts differ from other contemporary forms of spectacle and of writing, but also how the early modern mode of theatrical production, as exemplified primarily in the large amphitheaters, involved material practices which themselves have ideological implications.

As will by now be clear, this book participates in the broad-based movement in Renaissance studies over the last decade to cross the line which traditionally has separated the study of literature from the study of the political life of the culture which produced it.[3] Despite the differences dividing Marxist, new-historicist, and various feminist practices, a crucial premise uniting the work of all these groups is that no textual production simply gives an objective, impartial, or true account of the world. To *re*present the world is precisely to present it from a vantage point in contest with other vantage points. While it may be extremely difficult to specify the interests served by a particular representation, it is impossible for a political criticism to imagine a representation not implicated in the power relations of a particular society. Consequently, in my analysis of discourses of the theater, I begin by asking the crucial question: *cui bono?* Whose interests are served by particular discourses about or representations of theater and theatrical practice? My intent is to supplement moral questions – how does a text morally code, and render ethical judgment upon, particular instances of theatrical practice? – by political questions – what interests are served and what power relations constituted by such representations? From a political framework it becomes problematic simply to ask, as Philip Edwards, for example, has done, whether Shakespeare "approved" of theatrical deceit and trickery (1978: 115–25). Predictably, having examined a number of Shakespeare's deceptive villains and deceiving "healers," Edwards concludes that Shakespeare sometimes did and sometimes didn't approve of deceit, but on balance was more skeptical than accepting. This conclusion, of course, constructs Shakespeare as a good liberal with a hardworking conscience which made him wary of the very trade in which his dyer's hand had been dipped.

One problem with this analysis lies in trying to infer from a collection of dramatic scripts a unified authorial intention about anything. More importantly, this formulation of the question – did Shakespeare, in the abstract, approve of theatrical "deception"? – eclipses the possibility of asking how gender, class, race, and social marginality or centrality impinge on the way characters are depicted as bearers of theatrical power. Politics, and social stratification, complicate morality. In a culture where opportunities for self-fashioning were multiplying, not all forms of theatrical "playing" were equally sanctioned, which was the obvious point of my examination of Jorden's *A Briefe Discourse of a Disease called the Suffocation of the Mother* and a point one could illustrate repeatedly from the texts of Renaissance culture. The Malvolios of the age, upstart "crows" aspiring to act the part of the nobility, were less encouraged in their activities than were the courtiers who flaunted themselves and their gorgeous attire before the eyes of an aging queen, playing out scripts of courtship and courtiership in which their acting of a part signified, not social transgression, but accommodation to the fantasies and political strategies of the powerful.[4]

This study also differs from, but is obviously indebted to, the many metadramatic studies of the last several decades which have also noted the plethora of actors, audiences, and artist figures found in Renaissance plays (Calderwood 1971 and 1979; Egan 1972; Fly 1976; Homan 1981; Huston 1981; Righter 1962; Winny 1968). By and large, metadramatic criticism assumed that the presence of such figures signaled the drama's self-reflexivity, its articulation of an implicit *ars poetica* within its own texts. As James Calderwood succinctly stated: "Shakespeare's plays are not only about the various moral, social, political, and other thematic issues with which critics have so long and quite properly been busy but also about Shakespeare's plays" (1971: 5). To some extent it is undoubtedly true that Renaissance drama was strongly self-regarding. The secular public theater was a relatively new institution in Renaissance culture, and the plays produced for that theater reflect a heightened self-consciousness about what it means to create fictions, to manipulate audiences, and to negotiate between the lived world and discursive representations of it.

However, such criticism, with its inherently formalist and allegorizing bent, can obscure the extent to which the theater shared a discourse of theatricality with the larger culture. Louis Montrose shrewdly suggested this possibility some time ago when he argued that the drama's incessant preoccupation with dramatic practices did not so much indicate theatrical narcissism as the widespread emergence of a "dramatistic sense of life" resulting both from the secularization of Renaissance culture and from the social changes, including heightened social mobility, attendant upon the prolonged and uneven transition from feudalism to capitalism (1980b: 51–7; also Agnew 1986). These changes unsettled identities and social positions, encouraging, for better or worse, the sense that in some fundamental way men and women were actors in a self-scripted theater and must forge the identities once taken for granted.

Missing, however, from Montrose's account is a full analysis of the fierce struggles surrounding the social changes coincident with the emergence both of antitheatrical polemic and a dramatistic sense of life. Social mobility, unmooring people from their fixed identities and fixed stations, was a fact in the period, but a troubling one, as was the emergence of protocapitalist economic practices. Many of the most powerful social institutions of church and state were invested in maintaining an official ideology of stasis and fixed identity, if not for themselves, then for those whose mobility or theatrical self-fashioning they found troubling. As David Underdown writes: "In the century before 1640 the country had undergone a social and economic transformation while retaining a static theory of society to which these changes could not be accommodated" (1987: 9). My intent will be to use the representation of theatrical practices as one way of discussing the social struggles generated by the dual facts of massive social change and equally massive resistance to its acknowledgment.

This book, then, I see as part of a collective effort to resituate the study of Renaissance drama in an explicitly political framework and to transgress the boundaries often erected between the political world and those texts designated literary.[5] In part this has meant developing new reading strategies which, instead of focusing on the putative aesthetic "unity" of texts, have instead emphasized the contradictory elements of a text and the traces of the social struggles – political, ideological, economic – through which it emerged (Belsey 1980: 103–9; Venuti 1989: 3–14). As is by now widely recognized, certain key texts of the early moments of new historicism saw Renaissance theater simply as the servant of state power and as a mechanism for the production and/or reproduction of aristocratic ideology. In a famous essay, "Invisible Bullets," Stephen Greenblatt argued that on the Renaissance stage subversion was produced only to be contained in a way that glorified and helped to sustain the dominant power structures of Elizabethan England (1988: 21–65).

This position has quite rightly been critiqued from several quarters. Jonathan Goldberg, for example, writing from a Derridean perspective, has argued that language will not admit of the perfect containment of its subversive, destabilizing, endlessly "differing" possibilities. The dream of such containment is a totalitarian fantasy (1987: 242–64). Stephen Orgel, focusing on Elizabethan and Jacobean theatrical pageantry, has stressed the degree to which even artistic productions explicitly designed to honor the monarch could challenge or undermine his or her authority. As Orgel writes: "Theatrical pageantry, the miming of greatness, is highly charged because it employs precisely the same methods the crown was using to assert and validate its authority" (1985: 19–25 at 23). Theatrical power was thus not only used to create good subjects for absolutist monarchy, but to subject the king to the fashioning powers of the playwright. Power relations were reversed or challenged even as they were apparently affirmed.[6] At the same time Marxist and feminist critics have pointed out that assuming the theater's recuperative function precludes examining the possibility of its role in social change and contestation, just as focusing upon the monarch and the court as the starting point for analysis often precludes focusing on women and non-elite social groups (Belsey 1985a; Boose 1987; Cohen 1987; Dollimore 1984; Holstun 1989; Howard 1991a;

Neely 1988; Waller 1987; Wayne 1987). In short, certain forms of new-historicist analysis unintentionally made love to power, assigning to it an efficacy which in reality it could probably never achieve.

While I will be examining male-authored texts in this study, I will in large measure focus on how they presented women and non-elite social groups: servants, rogues and vagabonds, class aspirants, monarchical pretenders, and London citizens. In short, my focus will primarily be on those most insistently subjected to discursive, economic, and political control. While I do not underestimate the role of the public stage in reinforcing hierarchical social relations in Renaissance culture, I will, however, argue that the theater's role in culture was more complex than simply affirming masculine and aristocratic power. Neither *essentially* subversive nor recuperative, the institution could and did serve a variety of competing class and gender interests. In later chapters I will explore the specific conditions under which the theater advanced some interests and marginalized others. At the moment, however, I want to suggest several *general* reasons why this institution managed to be more than the captive of dominant power interests and why its ideological effectivity cannot therefore be formulaically predicted.

The ideological volatility of the Renaissance public stage stems directly from the kind of material institution it was and its place, literal and symbolic, in urban London in the late sixteenth and early seventeenth centuries. Steven Mullaney has written brilliantly about the significance of the fact that the public theaters were mostly located in the suburbs, in the liminal zone just beyond the direct control of the City Fathers (1988a: esp. 1–59). From this marginal position, he argues, the stage was able to embody and negotiate among a variety of competing ideological interests, rather than being the captive of only one. But more, of course, was involved than geography. For example, though the scripts for this theater were censored by that office of the Master of the Revels, and so implicitly were expected to conform to monarchical prescriptions, actual performances involved much more than rehearsing the words of the script. Irreverent clowning, improvisation, and bawdy gestures were all potential ways, on the stage, to make the enacted drama a more complicated ideological phenomenon than a perusal of the censored script might suggest (Bristol 1985; Weimann 1978).

Moreover, the theater was, despite revisionist arguments about its privileged auditors (Cook 1981), in some important sense a popular institution which offered an urban substitute for a rural popular culture increasingly under attack by Puritans and subject to restrictions by the state (Burke 1978: esp. 207–53; Hill 1964: esp. 145–258). The audience was mixed, including women as well as men, sailors, tradesmen, merchants, as well as courtiers and gentry visiting London from the countryside (Gurr 1987: esp. 49–79). As Walter Cohen has persuasively argued, this theater was a crucial meeting point for diverse social groups and for diverse discursive and performance traditions, both elite and popular in nature (Cohen 1985: esp. 17–19). While, of course, part of the work of theater could be to harmonize diversity and to present social divisions as natural rather than the product of man-made and unequal social arrangements, I will argue that the juxtaposition of diverse discourses and performance traditions at the site of the public stage could also expose the interestedness of particular ideological positions and open space for the production of new ideological positions and new modes of subjectivity. Of particular importance in this regard is the possibility that, in such a complex institutional setting, the ideological import of a dramatic fable and the ideological implications of the material conditions in which it was produced and consumed could conflict, interpellating subjects in contradictory ways that open space for change.

In short, I am going to argue the materialist case that in order to understand the ideological function of Renaissance theater one must attend – not just to the ideological import of dramatic narratives considered as if they were the equivalent of a printed prose tale – but also to the whole ensemble of practices attendant upon theatrical production at the public theater. That means one has to pay attention to the specifics of this site of ideological production and reproduction. If, for example, theatrical fictions circulated patriarchal ideology, on the stage men played women's parts in these fictions and transgressively assumed the garments and gestures of the other sex. Moreover, those who came to the theatres did so as spectators and auditors, not as readers; they took their theatrical pleasure in huge public buildings, not in solitary chambers; what was consumed there were works often collaboratively written, many of which never saw print. To the extent that the theater therefore continued to be linked to popular non-print culture and to function as an urban substitute for declining or suppressed rural pastimes, to that extent it seemed anathema to some members of the emerging bourgeoisie with its time-conscious, individualistic, entrepreneurial subjectivity (Fraser 1970: 52–76). The standard picture of an alliance of crown and popular theater against the attacks of Puritan reformers and City Fathers thus has a kind of logic. But the place of the public theater in the Elizabethan/Jacobean social formation is hardly so simple, in part because, I will argue, whatever its "intentions," the public theater helped call into being the very bourgeois subjectivity to which it was supposedly opposed. Attendants at the theater were not participants in a religious event or social ritual, but paying customers and spectators positioned to judge, as well as applaud, the fictions played out before them. As spectators became spectators rather than participants, judges rather than actors, the chances increased for seeing dramatic representations *as* representations, and not as mirrors of truth (Sorge 1987: 238–9).

It is, moreover, only partly useful to think of the theater as an ideological state apparatus, that is, an institution for the discursive, non-violent control of social subjects in the interests of the ruling segments of society (Althusser 1971). The apparatus of state censorship and the occasional imprisonment of dramatists and actors for sedition indicate how state power could be brought to bear on theatrical products and the producers of them. Yet censorship was often a hit-or-miss affair,[7] and the very need for periodic clampdowns indicates that the theater did not automatically or invariably do the work of promoting the interests of those vested with the authority to regulate its fictions. The urban marketplace, increasingly demanding the diversification of theatrical fare to accommodate the interests and tastes of mixed audiences, exerted its own pull on this institution, disrupting the cultural hegemony of king and court, putting in circulation cultural narratives that in some cases displaced or rewrote those of dominant social groups. How else to explain a play such as Heywood's *Edward IV*, the first part of which was produced *circa* 1600, in which the monarch-centered, male-dominated history play is subjected to a thorough revisioning. In it London citizens displace the monarch as the primary actors in the nation's history and a criminalized, but then resanctified and long-suffering citizen wife, Jane Shore,

14

becomes the play's affective center. As far as we know, this play never provoked the censor's wrath. It is not overtly subversive, if by that one means directly critical of the institution of monarchy or of the social hierarchies that monarchy secures. The political force of the play is badly explained by a language of subversion and containment, since what it enacts is an appropriation and rewriting of an established dramatic genre in the interests of an emerging social group, rather than a direct assault on those whose interests that genre had formerly served. The event marks the theater's participation in social change and social struggle, but it does not, I would argue, articulate subversion.

The rest of this book sets out the evidence and arguments for the positions sketched in this introduction. The second chapter, " 'Sathans Synagogue': The theatre as constructed by its enemies," examines the many attacks on the stage written in the late sixteenth and early seventeenth centuries in order to see why the practices of the theater seemed such a danger to many of Shakespeare's contemporaries and what it was about the institution that violated those common-sense assumptions which comprised the ideological horizons of the attacking groups. Moreover, I want to explore the ways in which antitheatrical polemic aimed in the first instance at the theater itself and at actors and stage plays crops up in other polemical sites and becomes, in effect, a general discourse of marginalization.

Part of the argument of the book is that stage plays themselves participated – through the representation of theatricality – in the cultural production of gender and class difference and in the production of cultural "centers" and "margins." To begin to work out in what sense this is true, the third chapter of the book, "Antitheatricality Staged: The workings of ideology in Dekker's *The Whore of Babylon* and Shakespeare's *Much Ado About Nothing*," looks at the way these two plays replicate, though in quite different ways and with quite different consequences, some of the premises of the antitheatrical tracts. While Dekker's violently anti-Catholic drama employs an antitheatrical discourse to demonize Catholics and foreigners, it does so in a manner that, rather than concealing the interested nature of its representations, reveals it. The result is ironically to undermine the ideological effectiveness of the play by making the workings of ideology visible. By contrast, *Much Ado About*

Nothing performs much more seamlessly the task of presenting interested representations of the real as if they were objective truth. The play resembles the antitheatrical tracts in its silent legitimation of the theatrical practices of the powerful and the demonization of those same practices in the hands of subordinated social groups, in this instance, women and bastards. However, even this text does not offer its audiences entirely coherent and monolithic ideological positions. For example, while the play disciplines the theatricality of women and non-aristocratic males, it is acted by men and boys of low estate who make their living impersonating their social superiors in theatrical fictions. But contradictions exist at other levels also, as between the conflicting demands of male bonds and marriage bonds in the play. The first depends on believing in the inherent theatrical duplicity of woman; the second in believing in her truth. In short, the play is a location where conflicting discourses intersect, and a political reading practice can pry open the contradictions among them.

The fourth chapter, "The Materiality of Ideology: Women as spectators, spectacles, and paying customers in the English public theater," is a materialist analysis of why the public theater could at times promote the destabilization of dominant ideologies as much as it could uphold them. In this chapter I am particularly concerned to examine how the theater may have had a differential impact on various social groups. Women of the middling sort, those warned by Stephen Gosson at the end of his first attack on the stage to shun the theater, are one of the principal groups I examine to ask what might have been the impact upon them of attendance at the public theater.

The fifth chapter, "Power and Eros: Crossdressing in dramatic representation and theatrical practice," continues my investigation of the impact of theatergoing on women by looking at how the theater represented female crossdressing. In the antitheatrical tracts, assuming the garments of the other sex is presented as a distortion of nature, a theatrical practice that hides the truth of men and women's "real" natures and upsets the hierarchical social relations between them. I look at what ideological consequences follow from the *staging* of female crossdressing by an all-male acting company. One purpose of this chapter is to emphasize both that gender struggle must be regarded as a central, rather than a peripheral, aspect of social

16

struggle in the period. Another purpose is to show that representations of female crossdressing belie the adequacy of subversion and containment models for framing questions of social contest and social change. While plays of female crossdressing nearly always end in patriarchal marriages and to that extent place limits on the power and independence of their heroines, they simultaneously instantiate the figure of the speaking, plotting, roving, crossdressed woman ever more firmly in the period's repertoire of theatrical representations and so in its cultural imaginary. It is as if, for a time, the theater *must* speak the crossdressed woman, must discursively produce her and put her into cultural circulation with a vividness that undercuts easy assumptions about the eventual "containment" of the threat that figure poses. Moreover, if these plays mostly end by overtly channelling sexual energy into marriage, their sustained play with same-sex erotic attraction, both within their fictions and at the presentational level of the all-male acting company, disrupts the finality of heterosexual closure and the celebration of proto-bourgeois marriage practices as the dominant cultural mode of either affective bonding or social alliance. In short, these plays seek to master cultural contradictions of several sorts, and a language of containment and subversion only flattens and simplifies their complex mediations of social change.

The sixth chapter, "Kings and Pretenders: Monarchical theatricality in the Shakespearean history play," examines the history play as a textual practice complexly concerned with legitimating the institutions of nation-state and absolutist monarchy emerging from the dissolution of the feudal settlement. In this process of legitimation, part of the work of the history play is to rewrite, in the discourse of statecraft, the theatrical practices undergirding the acquisition and exercise of monarchical power, and to separate these from the "mere theatricality" of imposters, rebels, and failed monarchs. In this process the history play repeatedly activates cultural equations between the "merely theatrical" and the feminine and the illegitimate. However, the instability of this process of monarchical legitimation is underscored in later history plays such as *Henry V* and Ford's *Perkin Warbeck* when, under conditions of modernity, actorliness can no longer be construed as the antithesis of kingliness, but as its founding condition.

As a whole this project attempts to give an account of why

the theater and theatrical practices were such objects of debate and contestation in early modern England and to see the place of theatrical discourse in that period's larger network of class and gender struggles. In opposition to certain gender-blind Marxist analyses of the period and the theater, I argue that the regulation of gender relations was a key element both in the antitheatrical debates and in the larger power struggles of early modern England. In opposition to certain new historical readings of the stage, I argue that the public theater was something other than an agent of the state, of the aristocracy, and of men. In its representations of theatrical practices and in its embodiment of theatrical power, the stage could, at times, challenge aristocratic and androcentric mappings of the world, opening space for the ideologies of the middling sort and for the negotiation of women's place in early modern culture. This book thus defines the Renaissance public theater as a vehicle for ideological contestation and social change and suggests that in this period theatrical power was real power, its control and regulation both an important political goal and, in the commercial marketplace, something of an impossibility.

At the outset it is probably well to state that the historicist project I am undertaking, that is, the attempt to achieve an understanding of the political force of Renaissance theatrical fictions at their original moment of production, can only be an impure and highly mediated undertaking. I am writing from within twentieth-century discourses and motivated by a set of political commitments, largely Marxist and feminist in nature, which structure and determine the questions I ask about the early modern period and about its dramatic and polemical texts. Certainly one can ask other questions and produce a different kind of knowledge of these texts. But social struggle occurs across the social formation, and at the level of knowledge production in the academy it often takes the form precisely of a struggle over the kinds of questions one asks, the kinds of knowledge deemed legitimate to produce. Literature, and especially a figure such as Shakespeare, is often still used as an example of what lies above or beyond political struggle and historical particularity. In presenting human nature, it presents what is and what must be. I argue another case, that what appears immutable and natural is changeable and man-made, and that though the signs of struggle are often effaced or ignored, texts are produced and read in conditions of contest (Howard and O'Connor 1987: 1–17). And the contests over texts are not merely trivial. Reading practices authorize other practices, instantiate systems of intelligibility that displace others. To place literature above ideology, rather than within it, makes it easier to read *The New York Times*, *Fatal Attraction*, or *The Congressional Record* in the same way.

A political criticism such as this book represents has, of course, come under fire from the strong conservative voices empowered in the Reagan–Bush era who see the politicizing and pluralizing of cultural study as endangering the primacy of the Anglo-American tradition and spoiling aesthetic pleasures by inquiring into art's social function.[8] William Bennett, Lynne Cheney, and Allan Bloom are not negligible powers in this society. An alternative pedagogy and critical practice must counter theirs, committed to the belief that a more just society emerges *from* diversity and not *in spite of* it, from the *dispersion* of power and not from its *consolidation* in the hands of a few.

Yet a left political criticism faces other obstacles as well as overt attacks from a culturally and politically powerful right. These include sectarianism (historicism *vs.* feminism, for example) and the professionalization of academic work in ways that make the expression of certain passions and commitments seem naive. Committed leftist criticism has been called self-righteous and moralizing, a new Puritanism obsessed with political "correctness." While no one, including myself, likes to be called a Puritan, it is useful to think about what practices are being policed by use of this word. If all criticism has political implications in that it turns its attention to one set of issues and not to others, makes certain questions have priority and not others, then the crucial difference is between a critical practice that acknowledges its commitments and one that does not. Strong adherence to one's beliefs is hardly the province of any one mode of knowledge production. But critics operating within the dominant thought systems of a culture can appear to be above ideology and above unseemly commitments because they speak from the unmarked position of that historically and culturally specific form of ideology to which the label common sense is often given. That is how ideological hegemony works. It trades on its dominance to make its own interested and partial positions seem to coincide with the natural, with common sense, with what goes without saying (Eagleton 1991: 5–6, 58–61).

By contrast, a criticism aimed at questioning the "truth to nature" of any paradigm of knowledge production must mark and make visible the location from which its own criticism issues. By location I do not mean identity position, but the discursive and political nexus which mandates that certain categories of analysis, certain questions, receive priority over others. Such marking serves not only to call attention to the interested, socially situated, condition of all knowledge-making projects; it also opens particular positions to critique, to an examination of their adequacy to their object of investigation and also to the urgencies and possibilities of the historical moment in which they are produced.[9] Any adequate and vital intellectual practice will not only have to reconstitute and rethink itself against the challenges of other projects of knowing, but against its own ideologically and historically induced inadequacies (Resnick and Wolff 1982: 44).

As an evolving mode of politicized knowledge production, feminism stunningly reveals the centrality of ongoing critique to the intellectual vitality of its project. For example, in the States liberal feminism has done much to make patriarchal oppression visible and to begin to combat its practices. Yet the critiques of lesbians, women of color, and working-class women have been essential in exposing the limitations of liberal feminism, its blindness to the plural nature of "woman," for example, and its inattention to the role of race and class in subjecting many women to forms of oppression different from those experienced by middle-class white women. One could give many examples of the ways in which Marxist feminists and psychoanalytic feminists and radical feminists have, through a process of ongoing critique and contestation, constantly pressed for the development of more sophisticated analyses of gender oppression and the development of new forms of redress and resistance. In such a context, stating the position from which one writes, and the telos guiding one's work, in no sense guarantees rigid adherence to an unchanging mode of analysis. Quite the contrary, it makes it available for critique and modification as part of an ongoing collective project.

As Donna Haraway has written, we all make knowledge from situated positions that reveal not our triumphant individuality, but our subjection to and empowerment by particular social practices and discourses (1988: 575–99). To work avowedly within a situated project of knowing affirms affiliation, one's indebtedness to collectively generated traditions of thought and action. It also means eschewing claims to see everything as if one were located outside of history, as if one were omniscient, disembodied. This is what Haraway rightly calls the old Enlightenment "god trick," the fiction that one can see "everywhere from nowhere" (1988: 581) and so be accountable for nothing. It is, of course, a trick favored by all who would make their situated and partial perspectives synonymous with objectivity and truth.

To acknowledge my commitment to Marxist feminism marks my situatedness as a producer of knowledge, and it affirms my affiliations with an ongoing project of social change. It does not, of course, absolve me from the labor of making a good case, of creating an argument accountable to internal standards of coherence and adequacy to the "facts" as they are known. Political criticism is synonymous with shoddy criticism only in the minds of its detractors. Moreover, acknowledgment of my commitment to Marxist feminism can not save me and others connected to this tradition of thought and action from the labor of constantly rethinking and reshaping the possibilities of that tradition so that it will remain adequate to emergent conditions. There is no way to get the analysis right "for all time." Only a profoundly ahistorical and individualistic culture could find that thought frightening. Perhaps one of the unforeseen benefits of the present emphasis on the cultural construction of the subject will be a new acceptance of the proposition that not even our thoughts and emotions are really and properly "our own." Perhaps therefore we can forget the anxious regard and guarding of that illusory self and learn instead to imagine, and to realize, new forms of the collective good.

2

"SATHANS SYNAGOGUE"
The theater as constructed by its enemies

The commercializing culture which sustained the development of the public theater in early modern England also sustained a vigorous polemical literature, some of it taking the theater as one of its primary objects of attack. In this chapter I examine some of the antitheatrical tracts produced between the opening of the commercial theaters in 1576 and their closing in 1642. In these tracts the theater, which through its scripts and spectacles daily represented imagined worlds to its beholders, itself became an object of representation over whose meaning and value various partisans engaged in heated discursive struggle. In the process certain distinctive narratives about this institution were developed, as well as a dense tropology of denigration and praise by which to define its worth and social effects. In this chapter I look at how these tracts rendered the emergent institution of the theater intelligible, but I will also examine the silences, contradictions, and rhetorical sleights of hand by which this polemic revealed its own implication in the social and ideological struggles of Tudor and Stuart England.

Antitheatrical tracts, of course, did not provide "objective" accounts or descriptions of how the Renaissance public theaters functioned. In fact, it has several times been suggested to me that these bits of mad polemic are irrelevant to the serious study of Renaissance theater since their derogations of theatrical practice are (1) obviously formulaic and ideologically motivated; (2) sometimes drawn from classical sources when not (3) drawn from other Elizabethan antitheatrical tracts; and (4) sometimes subordinated to a concern with social issues having no direct bearing on the theater *per se*. All this is true but does not deter me, since I am not engaging these tracts as descriptive documents, but as ideological productions designed to master or to mask contradictions in the social and economic life of the culture in which they were produced. The very fact that antitheatrical tracts were so wide-ranging, that they often constituted general anatomies of social folly, suggests that the public theater was not viewed in the period as an isolated phenomenon, but as part of an ensemble of cultural and social changes disturbing enough to warrant various forms of intervention and management. Through a symptomatic reading of these tracts, I hope to tease out what was feared, and by whom, about specific aspects of social change in the late sixteenth century, of which the emergence of the public theater in 1576 stood, for the polemicists, as instructive synecdoche. Moreover, I do not find it surprising that those directly involved in the social conflicts of the period had – when considered from my vantage point nearly four hundred years later – an imperfect understanding of the events of which they were a part. I will therefore argue that while the theater played a role in the social changes of the period, it was not quite the role the antitheatricalists assigned to it.

One falsely anthropomorphizes texts by describing them as "anxious," implying that they have psyches capable of displaying neurotic symptoms, yet I want to call the antitheatrical tracts a genre of anxiety to suggest something about the level of barely suppressed anger, fear, and intolerance that characterize their depictions of the practices and the social groups they attack. The anxiety, properly speaking, is a social, not a textual property, manifesting itself in displays of vituperation, denigration, and scapegoating typical of this genre. In particular, I want (1) to trace the connections repeatedly forged between theatrical practices and threats to established gender and class hierarchies and (2) to examine the truly astonishing selectivity of these tracts' condemnation of theatricality. Paradoxically, enemies of the theater could not seem to escape being proponents of certain forms of theatrical practice. Their moral condemnations of all theatricality were thus often transformed into complicated political discriminations between marked and unmarked, illegitimate and acceptable, modes of theatricality.

To begin to address the politics of these tracts and the terms in which they made sense of the theater, I begin with John

Northbrooke's *A Treatise wherein Dicing, Dauncing, Vaine Playes or Enterluds . . . are reproved*. Written in 1577 by a nonconformist preacher with Puritan leanings, this tract constructs the theater as one of an ensemble of institutions and practices destroying the religious and social fabric of England. Northbrooke stages the tract as a dialogue between an old man coming from church and a young man who has missed services because of his dedication to a life of idle pastimes, the worst of which are playgoing, dicing, and dancing. As Martha Rozett has argued (1984: 15–25), in the late sixteenth century preachers and playwrights often competed for audiences, especially before the banning of Sunday theatrical performances in 1583. For a time, at least, the church and the theater were posited as symbolically opposed places. And much of Northbrooke's tract is an angry fantasia on what it means to abandon the former place for the latter, old ways for new. In this discussion, the old man becomes the repository for vanishing values, the young man the example of the degenerate present.

Above all else, the theater in Northbrooke's schematization stands for idleness, the effects of which are readily apparent to him in the vast increase of vagrants, masterless men, and degenerate gentlemen throughout England. Some of Northbrooke's declamations against idleness are extremely colorful. While he can simply say that "to be idle and doe no good, is against the law of God and the law of nature" (Div), he is more likely, drawing upon Ecclesiastes, to cry out that "A slothfull man is to be compared to the dung of Oxen, and everye one that taketh it up, will shake it out of his hande: he is like a filthie stone, which every man mocketh at for his shame" (Hii); moreover, Northbrooke urges that coercion of a strong sort should be used against the idle. "Nourish not among you these idle loitering persons, but compell them with very hunger to labour: wherby you may learn, none ought to live idelly, but should be given to some vocation or calling to get his living withall, that he maye doe good unto others also" (Eiv^v). He is especially delighted by the rigor of Elizabeth's statutes to the effect that "idle vagrant and maisterlesse persons, that used to loiter, and woulde not worke, shoulde for the first offence have a hole burned through the gristle of one of his eares of an inche compasse. And for the seconde offence committed therein, to be hanged" (Hii). He goes on to say:

If these and such like lawes were executed justlye, truly, and severely (as they ought to be) without any respect of persons, favour or friendshippe, this dung and filth of ydlenesse woulde easily be rejected and cast oute of this Common wealth, there woulde not be so many loitering idle persons, so manye Ruffians, Blasphemers, and Swinge Buckelers, so many Drunkardes, Tossepottes, Whooremaisters, Dauncers, Fidlers, and Minstrels, Diceplayers, and Maskers, Fencers, Theeves, Enterlude players, Cutpurses, Cosiners, Maisterlesse Servauntes, Jugglers, Roges, Sturdye Beggers, counterfaite Egyptians, etc. as there are, nor yet so manye Plagues to bee amongst us as there are, if these dunghilles and filthe in Commonweales, were remooved, looked unto, and cleane caste oute, by the industrie, payne, and travell of those that are sette in authoritie, and have governemente.

(Hii)

In this diatribe against idleness, the public theater figures prominently, both because the actors who perform there, having in Northbrooke's eyes no legitimate vocation, are no better than masterless men whatever their tenuous connection to an aristocratic patron. And the audience who watched them perform is in his view equally sunk in idleness and sensuality. Speaking specifically in reference to the building of The Theatre and The Curtaine, he says, "I am persuaded that Satan hath not a more speedie way and fitter schoole to work and teach his desire, to bring men and women into his snare of concupiscence and filthie lustes of wicked whoredome, than those places and playes, and theaters are; And therefore necessarie that those places and Players shoulde be forbidden and dissolved and put downe by authoritie, as the Brothell houses and Stewes are" (Jii-Jii^v). And in a move that is to become normative, he especially warns women from the theater since there, removed from the safe enclosures of home, they are laid open to the gaze, and the lust, of many men, and become themselves inflamed by promiscuous gazing: "what safegarde of chastitie can there be, where the woman is desired with so many eyes, where so many faces looke upon hir, and againe she uppon so manye? She must needes fire some, and hir selfe also fired againe, and she be not a Stone" (Jiv).

25

As one of the early attacks on the theater, Northbrooke's diatribe establishes some of the conventions of the genre: namely, nostalgic longing for a lost and better past; fear that the popularity of "playing" reveals an erosion of cultural discipline and a legitimation of "idleness"; anxiety about the sensory stimulations of theatrical experience; and anger at those, such as women and actors, no longer in their proper places of subordination, i.e. their husbands' houses or their lords' great halls, but situated in the dangerously open and lawless space of the public theater. Later tracts will advance their arguments with greater philosophical rigor and will focus less on the evils of Sunday playing, which was banned in the 1580s, but most employ Northbrooke's basic premise that the theater, as Satan's school, signals the degeneracy of a nation in which men and women have lost the will to work and have wandered from their fixed stations and vocations.

Northbrooke's anxiety about idleness, of course, responds to some real changes in social and economic relations in sixteenth-century England, but he unerringly mistakes effects for causes and relentlessly moralizes phenomena having economic and political causes and, hence, economic and political cures. A. L. Beier and others have shown that in sixteenth-century England fewer and fewer people had fixed manorial ties. Consequently, the wage-labor pool grew, creating a class of landless persons alien from the feudal world of obligation and fixed residence, but with no clear stake in the emerging bourgeois world of discipline and self reliance (Beier 1985: xxi; see also Clark and Soudern 1988). Often wandering the roads in pursuit of seasonal work, these vagrants and "masterless men" were the target of a series of state measures designed to regulate their movements and behaviors. A 1531 statute ordered vagrants to be carted and whipped until bloody; in 1572 they were directed to be flogged and to have holes bored in their ears (Beier 1985: 159). (This seems, in fact, to be the statute of which Northbrooke so enthusiastically approves in his tract.) An elaborate system of licenses and passports was developed to control the movements of the poor, a system which ironically encouraged a growing market in "counterfeit" passes and licenses. All of this social legislation reached its culmination in the Elizabethan Poor Laws of the late 1590s with their strict separation of the able-bodied from the "deserving" poor (Beier 1983).

These social factors help to explain the virulence of North-brooke's animus against "the idle" and the strong associations he forges between the dissolution of established social order and the eruption, like a boil, of an institution such as the public theater where it seems to him the idle congregate to be frivol-ously entertained by counterfeiters. In a strong sense, place for Northbrooke determines identity. People at the theater are not *where* they should be (i.e. in their parishes, at work or at worship); consequently, they are not *who* they should be, but are released into a realm of Protean shapeshifting with enormous destabilizing consequences for the social order. Northbrooke and many subsequent antitheatricalists, along with those devising new statutes to regulate vagrancy, are obsessed with *re*marking and *re*situating the bodies of "the idle" and "the unmastered." The desire to return the poor to their parishes of origin is consonant with a desire to put their bodies in churches, not theaters, on Sundays. The impulse to bore a hole in the ear of vagrants, so that their social status will be instantly recognizable, is consonant with the desire to enforce sumptuary laws.

Foucault was brilliantly acute when, at the beginning of *Discipline and Punish* he argued that a dominant form of absolutist power was the power to inscribe the body with visible marks of its subjection (Foucault 1979: esp. 54–7). In the social context of sixteenth-century England, the material manifestations of such power included the full panoply of regulations and discursive exhortations by which the bodies of "the idle" become objects of scrutiny, certainly, but also objects to be *re*positioned and *re*inscribed within the literal and symbolic geography of the Commonwealth. From Northbrooke on, antitheatrical tracts connect the theater with social subjects who by being out of their appropriate places of work and worship have lost their proper social identity and become dung (inhuman) or counterfeits (mannekins falsely occupying another's proper place). Theatergoing thus becomes connected with the loss or confusion of identity, but also with usurpation, seizing a social position which one does not, by one's birth, deserve, aspiring to an identity which can therefore be discredited as illusory, counterfeit, deceptive. Antitheatrical polemic is one apparatus for policing transformations of social identity by specific groups of Elizabethan social subjects. As we shall see, this policing activity is often mediated through "aesthetic" debates about the relationship of truth to dramatic illusion.

It is important to remark at this point that Northbrooke's arguments are riddled with contradictions one can usefully probe to see how he himself is implicated in the social changes he condemns but, more importantly, which begin to suggest the ways in which the theater was a more complex phenomenon than the polemicists – or their pro-theater opposites – could consciously acknowledge. In regard to Northbrooke's own blind spots, I want to begin with a consideration of the strongly iconoclastic strain in his tract. Like many antitheatricalists, Northbrooke attacks the stage in part because it allures the senses, particularly the eye. It invites its spectators to love outward spectacles and turn aside from the inner illuminations of faith. Hearing sermons, rather than seeing plays, is what Northbrooke's old man proposes to his young companion. As Barish and others have pointed out, anti-Catholic and antitheatrical polemic converge in this period because in a strongly Protestant discourse such as Northbrooke's, the theater, like the Catholic Church, is constructed as committing its patrons to the worship of hollow idols: outward signs, not inward essences, things of the flesh, not of the spirit (Barish 1981: 161–6). Yet antitheatrical discourse is hardly self-consistent in regard to the regime of outward signs. Cheek by jowl with the attack on the idolatrous nature of theatrical representation is the simultaneous demand that the poor, the idle, and the feminine make themselves iconically legible, bear upon their persons – by clothing, by brands, by badges – marks of their subjection to what in the largest sense would make them "mastered" men and women: strict hierarchies of gender, class, and status.

In part because of the strongly iconoclastic bent of their writings, Renaissance antitheatricalists are often connected with "progressive" forces in Renaissance culture, i.e. with the emerging Puritan, merchant, and gentry interests that eventually coalesced to oppose hierarchy and "popishness" in the church and to strike against the iconic embodiment of state power, the monarch himself (Fraser 1970: 163–5). Yet progress *for whom* is the question. In their denigration and policing of the poor, the unemployed, and the feminine, these writers contribute to the oppression of disempowered social groups. This is partly a consequence of the antitheatricalists' participation in the construction of a distinctively Reformation ideology emphasizing hard work and the proper husbanding of time, a doctrine suited to the emergence of protocapitalist economic practices and to the regulation of the lives of a swelling urban populace and work force (Fraser 1970: 52–76; also Hill 1964: 124–218). Northbrooke's tract can be identified with an emergent middle-class ideology opposed, on the one hand, to the idleness of the traditional aristocracy, but, on the other hand, even more strongly opposed to the "idle" and "masterless" poor.[1] He berates gentlemen, for example, who do not, in a virile fashion, dedicate themselves to the physical, mental, and moral discipline required of the nation's leaders. He would have them engage in wrestling, running, and practice with the long bow, pastimes "used of olde time" (Liii^v). And he laments "For they suppose that it is no part belonging to their calling, for to heare sermons, pray, and studie for learning, nor to be exercised in heroicall actes and martiall affaires, but onely to hawke and hunt all day long" (Liv). Yet his recurring excremental images – his language of dung – are reserved for those at the bottom of the social scale, for those "masterless men" who in many cases had been cut loose from their traditional social positions by enclosure movements and other changes in the agrarian economy that were transforming the rural laborer into a precariously poised wage worker, and often into an indigent vagrant. The spokesperson for protocapitalist values of thrift, industry, and hard work shows little compassion for those who were hurt by transformations in the economic and social structure of rural life, blaming their economic displacement and destitution on moral failings.[2] In a move not unknown in our day, Northbrooke prescribes hard work as a cure for those who in many cases could undoubtedly find no work.

However much Northbrooke may sound like a spokesperson for an emergent social group, though, he does not recognize himself as such, but as a proponent of a simple return to past values and a past way of life less "degenerate" than the present. Made uneasy by many of the changes around him, Northbrooke overtly locates the alternative, not in new social arrangements, but in a return to a fixed feudal order that in some ways would be inimical to the values he promulgates through his praise of thrift and industry. It is not true, of course, that only an emergent middle class engaged in protocapitalist practices during this period. Members of the traditional aristocracy were participating in joint-stock companies, angling for monopolies, and engineering many of the agrarian reforms producing the wandering laborers Northbrooke despises and fears.[3] Elizabethan society was changing at the top, as well as at the middle and the bottom of the social formation. But a vast gulf still separated an aristocratic ideology of leisure and the markedly modern emphasis in Northbrooke's writing on work, thrift, and self-regulation.

The fear of disorder from below, however, mutes, in this early tract, the writer's critique of the traditional aristocracy. This same fear, I would argue, also causes him to misrecognize some of the potentialities of the theater itself. Worried about masterless men, Northbrooke condemns the theater as a seat of idleness without noting the actual industriousness of those who were erecting the new commercial pleasure palaces that would come to ring urban London and, in some cases, would become flourishing businesses and routes to social advancement for the hardworking entrepreneurs, like William Shakespeare, who labored within them. Moreover, he overestimates the extent to which it was the unemployed or the "masterless" who congregated at the London theaters. As Andrew Gurr has demonstrated, the theaters, especially the amphitheater houses, were patronized by all classes, though higher prices at the hall theaters meant they were more exclusively patronized by merchants, gentlemen, gentlewomen, and the aristocracy than were the amphitheaters (Gurr 1987: 49–79). While apprentices and students from the Inns of Court frequently attended the public theaters, the genuinely destitute would seldom have been able to afford even the cheapest penny admission. More importantly, the antitheatricalists' preoccupation with the theater's visual allure and with its potential to draw the poor further from a life of true faith and self-discipline, blocked any thought that the theater itself might breed a certain form of iconoclasm. On the one hand, the public theater was not overtly an iconoclastic or subversive institution. It trafficked in the seductions of the visual; it seldom overtly opposed the common sense of the aristocratic/monarchical bloc, though it depicted that bloc's repeated struggles to adapt to changing social circumstances and to the emergence of new class ideologies (Cohen 1985). This is probably why successive monarchs protected the theater and sometimes seem to have thought of it as a diversion to pacify and distract those very uprooted and potentially seditious subjects Northbrooke would submit to the pillory and the branding iron (Crewe 1986: 71–85).

Yet, as a number of contemporary critics have suggested, this theater had the power to alter spectators' *relationships* to both visual and verbal representations in potentially disruptive ways. The stage, for example, put certain privileged symbols such as representations of monarchy into broad cultural circulation. This stripped those symbols of their sacred aura, making it more possible for spectators to have a critical, rather than a merely reverential, attitude toward them (Kastan 1986; Mullaney 1988b). The iconoclastic potential of the theater, largely overlooked by monarch and antitheatricalist alike, thus lay at least in part in its ability to demystify certain privileged representations and to alter spectators' relationships to them. This stage made its spectators just that, spectators to and judges of – rather than ritual participants in – a highly self-conscious scene of representation (Righter 1962: 76–86).

The theater's ability to alter the ideological import or the social meanings of the narratives, symbols, and conventions it shared with the broader culture is the primary concern of later chapters in which I analyze specific play texts. My purpose here, however, is simply to suggest that the antitheatricalists did not necessarily see the ways in which the theater itself could foster the iconoclastic temper. It is not surprising that under the pressure of imperfectly understood social change, monarchs who befriended the theater did not recognize fully its potential to undermine or change the terms of monarchical, aristocratic, and masculine power, while iconoclasts who attacked the theater seemed not to have recognized its potential to promote a certain kind of iconoclasm, a skepticism about the representational order as synonymous with truth.

What the antitheatricalists *did* seem to recognize more clearly than their opponents was the disruptive effect of a burgeoning marketplace, in which the commercial theater was implicated, on traditional understandings of one's social "place." The sixteenth century was, of course, not only a time of increased poverty and enforced idleness for many of England's laboring poor, but it also saw the beginnings of what Joan Thirsk has called England's first "consumer society" (Thirsk 1978). The quickening of trade and the growth of industry meant an increase in the kinds and number of material articles to be bought and owned by those with the wherewithal to buy. The aristocracy, of course, had always had access to luxury goods, but sixteenth-century trade increased the range of such items available in London where the building of the New Exchange in 1609 came to symbolize the centrality of London as England's commercial center and of "shopping" as a privileged cultural activity (Fisher 1990; Newman 1991: 129–43). Even yeomen's houses in the sixteenth century bore the traces of enhanced access to new consumer goods such as knives, felt hats, buttons, copper thread, tobacco pipes, gloves, glass, and earthenware (Thirsk 1978: 128–9). Of course, this proliferation of goods could have destabilizing consequences upon the visual economy through which gradations of class and status were registered. Suddenly, some people could dress, eat, and live in a manner not entirely consonant with traditional expectations regarding their "place" in society. Moreover, imposters or "counterfeits" could usurp – by the questionable acquisition of finery – the rightful places of their betters. In tracts such as Phillip Stubbes's *The Anatomie of Abuses* published in 1583 we find the fear of idleness and of masterless men coupled to fears about the "counterfeitability" of social identity in a world in which the visible marks of status can be bought, sold, borrowed, or stolen.

Importantly, Stubbes begins his treatise by castigating excesses in apparel, supposedly because they signify the sin of pride. But moral outrage often signals political struggle, and clothing was a terrain where certain struggles over class and gender hierarchy were most obviously played out in late sixteenth-century England. Stubbes, like many antitheatricalists, was preoccupied with policing this highly politicized semiotic system. So was the state. One of the homilies appointed by Elizabeth to be read in churches at Sunday services was entitled "Against Excess of Apparel." In it parishioners are enjoined to remember their vocations "in as much as God hath appointed every man his degree and office, within the limits whereof it behoveth him to keep himself. Therefore all may not look to wear like apparel, but everyone according to his degree, as God hath placed him" (*Sermons* 1816: 260).[4] Excess in apparell offends not only God, but also the monarch. As the homily says, dress is now "so gorgeous, that neither Almightie God by his word can stay our

32

proud curiousity in the same, neither yet godly and necessary laws, made by our princes, and oft repeated with the penalties, can bridle this detestable abuse, whereby both God is openly contemned, and the prince's laws manifestly disobeyed, to the great peril of the realm" (258).

The worry seems to be that social distinctions are erased by indiscriminate acquisition of sartorial finery: distinctions, for example, between men and women, between chaste and modest women and whores, between gentlemen and commoners. The homilist laments "there is no difference in apparel between an honest matron and a common strumpet. Yea, many men are become so effeminate, that they care not what they spend in disguising themselves, ever desiring new toys, and inventing new fashions" (261–2). Exhortations from the pulpit to remember one's place and to signify it properly by one's dress were supplemented by sumptuary proclamations, directives which set forth what kinds of textiles, ornaments, furs, and even colors of clothing could be worn by men and women of various ranks. Of course, as Wilfred Hooper points out, these statutes always had a protectionist, as well as a sumptuary purpose. They protected the native cloth industry by barring widespread use of imported dyes and fabrics (Hooper 1915: 433–49). The antitheatrical writers, however, focused primarily on the social disruptions occasioned by sartorial excess. Ironically, by insisting that particular subjects express their real social identities by outward signs, the antitheatricalists and the state threatened to lay bare or make explicit the theatricality at the very heart of the traditional social order. Insisting that one's real social place and one's real nature are what matter, the antitheatrical tracts reveal that these things can only be expressed "theatrically," by recourse to the very materials (fabrics, colors, ornaments) with which actors and upstarts performed their self-transformative and deceptive magic (Barish 1981: 166–7).

Oblivious to such ironies, Stubbes throws himself wholeheartedly into the battle over dress. There is nothing tame or abstract in his condemnation of sartorial excess. Instead, ironically revealing the appeal of material adornment, he rails with great particularity against cork shoes, French hose, double stacks of starched ruffs, false hair, and oversized doublets. While the impracticality and exorbitant cost of these fashions outrage him, they signify a more fundamental evil: namely, these clothes are "more gorgeous, sumptuous and precious than our State, calling or condition of lyfe requireth" (Stubbes 1583: B7). They conceal the real conditions of a man's or a woman's existence and make them mere players who cannot be located in terms of rank or social station. As Stubbes says:

> there is such a confuse mingle mangle of apparell in Ailgna [England], and such preposterous excesse therof, as every one is permitted to flaunt it out, in what apparell he lust himselfe, or can get by anie kind of meanes. So that it is verie hard to knowe, who is noble, who is worshipfull, who is a gentleman, who is not.
>
> (C2ᵛ)

The streets of London provided one scene where this "mingle mangle" of apparel appalled the eye, but the theater was the place where such transgressions were literally institutionalized. There men of mean rank daily wore the clothes of noblemen – and worse, of women. Actors were thus the arch counterfeiters. But, by implication, their practices encouraged parallel transgressions in their audiences. In an interesting associational progression, Stephen Gosson, in his 1579 work, *The Schoole of Abuse*, writes:

> How often hath her Majestie with the grave advice of her honorable Councell, sette downe the limits of apparell to every degree, and how soone againe hath the pride of our harts overflowed the chanel? How many times hath access to Theaters been restrayned, and how boldly againe have we reentered?
>
> (Gosson 1579: C6)

To flout the sumptuary laws and to go to the theater are clearly connected in Gosson's mind, though on the face of it there is no necessary reason why audience members should mimic the actors in violating sartorial decorum. But the antitheatricalists obviously regarded the entire playhouse – pit, galleries, *and* stage – as an arena of visual display encouraging transgressive transformations of identity. In attacking those who attended the theater, as well as the institutions and its actors, Stubbes and Gosson were trying to deny Proteus his socially disruptive power, that is, were trying to stop the visible transformations of the self encouraged by the theater and the marketplace. Like

Northbrooke, they did so by championing the view that one's place in the hierarchical social order was determined by God and was, properly speaking, immutable.

Antitheatrical polemic thus becomes the reverse of the more positively nuanced rhetoric of Renaissance self-fashioning written about so suggestively by Stephen Greenblatt. As Greenblatt has argued, in certain Renaissance writings the ancient trope of man as actor comes to bear a new meaning (Greenblatt 1980: 1–3). No longer actors in a God-given script, individuals are presented as writing the scripts in which, through studious self-cultivation and artful self-presentation, they will perform.[5] The courtesy literature which became one site for authorizing this view of identity may well have been *intended* to stem social mobility by defining the traits by which a true gentleman was known. Ironically, what this literature revealed was that the characteristics of a gentleman were not inherent in any particular class, but were learnable, just as the clothing of a gentleman was buyable. Consequently, upstarts appropriated the lessons of this literature and used it to increase the very mobility it was intended to suppress (Whigham 1984: 5). Greenblatt is undoubtedly correct in arguing that the notion of infinite possibility such rhetoric promised was an illusion (Greenblatt 1980: 256); material and discursive forces constrained every act of "self-fashioning." But this doesn't mean that the language of self-fashioning was not culturally important as a justification of practices aimed at status transformations.

Stubbes, however, hates the very idea of theatrical self-fashioning, especially if it might in any way empower the disempowered. The great irony, of course, is that a prolific writer and public figure such as Stubbes could never quite escape being involved in the theatricalization of the self he rails against. To become a man of print, to create distinct writing personae, to enter the marketplace with one's writings were practices of self-transformation and self-fashioning which enhanced, rather than retarded, the commercialization of culture to which Stubbes was overtly opposed. Willy-nilly, he was caught in the whirligig of change, despite the fact he did not literally become a stage actor or court waterfly.

In this regard it is important to recognize that in antitheatrical tracts and in other forms of polemical writing with which they are linked, attacks on "shapeshifting" are nearly always highly selective. Certain groups, and not others, are the objects of these attacks. Northbrooke focuses on the counterfeiting ways of vagrants and masterless men; Stubbes gives a great deal of space to women. Clearly, a range of social struggles is mediated through antitheatrical rhetoric. While interclass conflicts are crucial, factors such as gender and religion complicate any attempt to reduce the terms of social struggle to a single axis. For Stubbes, women, like counterfeiting knaves and upstart crows, falsify their true identities by assuming apparel, manners, and social positions not truly their own. But for women, more than for other social groups, the convenient fiction is that such behavior is part of their "nature." They are the inherently theatrical and duplicitous sex with temperaments prone to change and inconstancy.

Women's dress, whether described as too mannish, too sumptuous, or too exotic, comes in for special attack, as does women's use of cosmetics, because both facilitate woman's supposed love of endless self-transformation. As Stubbes says, "Proteus that Monster could never chaunge him self into so many fourmes and shapes as these women do, belike they have made an obligation with hel and are at agreement with the devil, els they would never outrage thus" (F5). His rhetoric stresses distortion and adulteration. Women who wear men's clothes are characterized as "Hermaphroditi; that is, Monsters of bothe kindes, half women, half men" (F5^v). Women who wear great hoops and petticoats are "artificiall women" (F6^v), "puppits" (F6^v), or things so deformed they are hardly credited with life. There is considerable violence in this rhetoric: anger at women who exercise independence, who assume male prerogatives, who transform themselves by following fashion and not the laws of "kinde" or the sumptuary prescriptions. The anger not only signals male anxiety about the rule of a female sovereign, but also a more widespread gender tension indicated not only by an outpouring of literature defending and attacking women, but also by increases in many areas in disciplinary mechanisms such as the use of the cucking stool and charivaris.[6]

The terms of Stubbes's attack on Protean women are echoed over and over in the vast antifeminist literature that grew to a crescendo in the early seventeenth century. In 1615, Joseph Swetnam wrote *The Araignment of Lewde, idle, froward and unconstant women* which went into ten editions in the ensuing century (Hull

1982: 112). This "bear-bayting of women" (Swetnam 1615: A3ᵛ) insists, as do the antitheatrical tracts, on the fundamental duplicity of women, their inherent theatricality. Unlike Pico, who finds the idea of Protean man invigorating, Swetnam finds the idea of Protean woman terrifying. As he says: women "have Sirens songs to allure thee, and Xerxes cunning to inchaunt thee, they beare two tongues in one mouth like Judas, and two heartes in one breast like Magus, the one full of smiles and the other full of frownes, and all to deceive the simple and plain meaning men, they can with Satyer out of one mouth blow hot and colde" (B2ᵛ-B3). These grotesque images of female doubleness and duplicity draw on long traditions of misogynist thought, but the commercialization of late sixteenth- and early seventeenth-century London culture gave this rhetoric new purchase. In 1616 in *A Treatise Against Painting and Tincturing of Men and Women* Thomas Tuke rails at women who paint, who eschew modest dress, who alter their hair color and their complexion. As Tuke says, such a woman, "though shee do affect singularity, yet she loves plurality of faces" (K2). "Not truths, but shadowes of truths shee is furnisht with; with seeming truths, and with substantiall lies" (K3). Tuke is very specific about the material source from which flow the things women need to transform their persons. "London, London hath her heart. The Exchange is the Temple of her Idols. In London she buys her head, her face, her fashion" (K2ᵛ). Again one encounters a rhetoric of idolatry. Tuke connects women who fetishize the objects buyable in the marketplace, and so become alienated from their "true nature" and "true needs," with those who engage in other forms of idolatry.

For many in the period, the great fountainhead of idolatry and deceptive theatricality was the Roman Church. It is therefore no surprise when Tuke careens from a discussion of women who paint to a diatribe against the Catholic Church. As I have indicated elsewhere, such slippage from one object of attack to another is quite common in all these tracts. Disapprovingly, Tuke reports that Spanish priests encourage women to paint. He thunders:

> Surely it is a doctrine that doth well enough become the Jesuites, who as they are the great Masters of lying, equivocation, and mentall reservation, so doe they make no difficultie, to teach that it is lawfull to belie the face, and the

complexion. Secondly, it well enough beseemes the Church of Rome, who as shee is the Mother of spiritual fornications, magicke, sorcerie and witchcraft, so hath God given her over to defile her selfe with corporall polutions and fornications, not onely to give allowance to publike Stewes and Brothel-houses, but that the Masse it self (which is the master peece of the Papacie) shold be made the baude to much uncleannesse, as is well knowne by their Masses at midnight, and their morning Matins before day. And therfore this old romish Jesabel, as she hath painted her owne face with the faire shew of many goodly ceremonies, of antiquity and succession, and multitude of her professors, thereby to set the world at a gaze, so in this particular also she doth tollerate the abuses of her children.

(H^v)

The painted woman and the Catholic Church – itself personified as a painted woman – are interchangeably constructed. The duplicity of women is encouraged by priests because the whole Catholic religion is one of false piety and organized deception. Exactly what was supposed to go on at those midnight masses and daybreak matins Tuke only intimates – clearly sexual depravities of some sort. This is the type of double purpose repeatedly attributed to the theater, where, it was alleged, under the guise of entertaining or even educating the audience, actors, like priests, debauched and corrupted that audience, making women prey to young gallants and making men effeminate.

The political motivations behind and the selectivity of these outraged attacks on the vices of painting and self-transformation are sometimes hilariously obvious. At one point Tuke uses a wonderfully revealing extended metaphor. Overtly, he abhors all painting, acting, and artifice. Yet when he describes how a husband should wean a woman from painting, he does so in these terms:

Dost thou not see that painters, when they goe about to make a faire picture, doe new apply these colours, and then others, wiping out the former? Be not thou more unskilfull then painters. They being to paint the shape of the bodies on tables, do use so great paines and care; and is it not meet that wee should trie all conclusions, use all meanes, when we desire to make soules better? ... If by degrees thou shalt thus reforme thy wives mind, thou shalt be the best painter, a faithfull servant, an honest husbandman.

(F2)

Tuke's rhetoric is fascinating, since while condemning one form of painting (cosmetics), he condones another (the fashioning of a wife's soul to conform to her husband's wishes). The key point, of course, is who does the fashioning, for it is inherently an exercise of power. Women are not to do it themselves, for that shows their alliance with the devil, but men are free to shape this weaker sex as they may wish, for that is merely the natural order of things. In short, they wear the label of "painter" with a difference.

With Swetnam and Tuke I have, of course, turned aside for a moment from the antitheatrical tracts *per se* to glance at their polemical cousins, the antifeminist treatises. The two genres share, however, an overt essentialism about identity – an insistence that some behaviors distort and falsify the *true* nature and the *true* position (inevitably a subordinate position) of certain social groups – and both genres apply their strictures against theatricality selectively. Each plays a role, therefore, in the political management of what each identifies as a crisis of identity in the commercializing, uprooted world of sixteenth- and seventeenth-century England. Each attempts to conceal the ways the entire social order, and not just the "idle," "seditious," or "upstart" segments of it, are implicated in the practices of self-transformation they castigate.

In certain of the antitheatrical tracts, especially those that are not general anatomies of folly but focus more precisely on the theater and its modes of representation, the overtly political nature of the attack on social mobility and what are perceived as transgressions of hierarchy is mediated through an aesthetic debate about mimesis and the "truth" of representation. I want to argue, however, that even these "sophisticated" versions of the antitheatrical genre are deeply invested in managing social relations in Elizabethan and Jacobean England, and are not concerned solely with aesthetic questions. Politics and aesthetics are inevitably intertwined, especially as the antitheatricalists move to appropriate various forms of social authority to underwrite their views and give them the stamp of the natural. A powerful subtext in these tracts therefore concerns not just the morality or truth of theatrical representation, but who will have access to and control of the means of theatrical representation, both in the theater and outside it.

Stephen Gosson's 1582 tract, *Playes Confuted in Five Actions*, is one of the better-crafted and better-organized antitheatrical efforts. Its ironies begin, however, with its title, which uses the idea of the five-act structure of classical drama to wage war on the theater. In the body of the tract Gosson argues that plays tell lies about reality and satanically distort the truths of nature. Of the drama Gosson writes: "Plays are no Images of trueth, because sometime they handle such thinges as never were, sometime they runne upon truethes, but make them seeme longer, or shorter, or greater, or lesse then they were, according as the Poet blowes them up with his quill, for aspiring heades, or minceth them smaller, for weaker stomakes" (1582: D5-D5ᵛ). But the attack on theatrical distortions of reality quickly extends to an attack on the agents of theatrical representation, the actors, especially as they lie about their sex in taking on the garments of women: "The Law of God very straightly forbids men to put on womens garments, garments are set downe for signes distinctive betwene sexe and sexe, to take unto us those garments that are manifest signes of another sexe, is to falsifie, forge, and adulterate, contrarie to the expresse rule of the worde of God" (E3ᵛ).

Stubbes, who in *The Anatomie of Abuses* steals great pieces of Gosson's tract, takes Gosson's rhetoric about male actors dressing as women and uses it to attack women who at the theater or elsewhere dress mannishly or outlandishly: "Our apparell was given us as a signe distinctive to discern between sex and sex, and therefore one to weare the Apparel of another sex, is to participate with the same, and to adulterate the veritie of his own Kinde" (F5ᵛ). The progression is instructive. Theater is a form of representation particularly committed to the falsification of the real; actors are a category of beings prone, presumably by their unmastered state, to a willing promulgation and intensification of these lies by the counterfeiting of their identities through the assumption of the signs of another's sex and rank; any potentially disruptive social subject whose actions can be constructed as instances of transgressive shapeshifting can therefore be classed with the transgressive actor. The question, of course, is who has the power to determine whose practices will receive this categorization.

The question of authority haunts the antitheatrical tracts, often with paradoxical results. But it is a key issue, since the legitimacy of the world view constructed in the tracts depends for its material effectivity precisely on the degree to which it is perceived as authorized by state, religious, and learned authority, as well as supported by the repressive apparatuses of the state. In his attack on plays as lies and actors as liars, Gosson marshals a host of authorities both classical and biblical to support his position. In doing so he makes use, as do a number of writers arguing both for and against the theater, of tactics regularly employed in Elizabethan polemical debate. But the marshaling of authorities both authorizes his position and reveals it *as* authorized, as dependent on various forms of legitimation that can be, and were, disputed by writers on the other side of the question.

Particularly telling is Gosson's attempt to enlist the authority of Elizabeth on the antitheatrical side by constructing the battle over the theaters as a contest between God and the devil, Protestantism and Catholicism. He argues that the devil, faced with the virtue of Queen Elizabeth and the success of the Protestant Reformation, has to work more craftily than ever before. The devil's best instruments for sowing social discord are bawdy Italian books and stage plays. God is represented as desiring the banning of both. Of course, it wasn't God, but important figures in the City of London, who wanted the theater abolished.[7] The City was quite clear about its distaste for this upstart institution located just beyond the perimeter of its actual control. From this liminal zone the City constantly feared the outbreak of subversive or disruptive activity. This continued to be so right up to the time when parliament closed the theaters. Before that neither the monarch nor the privy council responded affirmatively to pleas from the City to shut the theater, though care was taken to license and censor stage productions. Moreover, Elizabeth, James, and Charles, each of whom resisted City pressure to suppress the theater and to varying degrees extended their own patronage to it, themselves employed highly theatrical pageants, processions, and allegorical tableaux as part of the arts of statescraft.[8] Perhaps more surprisingly, the City, site of much of the outcry against the public theater, cultivated with great enthusiasm the theatrical pageantry of the Lord

Mayor's shows.[9] These facts suggest that while Gosson may talk about the stage as an object of struggle between God and the devil, the real contest of authorities was more mundane. Everyone recognized theater as a powerful and potentially dangerous force; the real questions were: who would control this power and which theatrical practices would be stigmatized, which ruled legitimate?

One of the most politically interesting attempts to lodge control over theatrical representation in the hands of a properly authorized elite is found in Sir Philip Sidney's urbane tract, *An Apology for Poetry* (1595). Unlike the other tracts I have been examining, Sidney's is ostensibly pro-art, even pro-theater. Yet his complicated defense of the stage is framed in terms which reveal fears of the usurpation of privilege by the unworthy, the elite's loss of control of the means of representing the real. Ironically, Gosson had dedicated his first attack on the theater to Sidney, trying to enlist the authority of this important Protestant aristocrat behind his cause. It may have been this treatise which prompted the composition of the quite antithetical *An Apology for Poetry*, in which Sidney ignores Gosson's attempt to abolish the public theater by royal fiat and defends poetry and the theater from the charge that poetic fictions are lies (Ringler 1942: 117–24; Kinney 1974: 44). "Now for the poet," Sidney writes, "he nothing affirms, and therefore never lieth" (Sidney 1595: 123). Instead, poetic fictions go beyond the world of fact and the arid prescriptions of philosophy to show what might and should be. Sidney thus counters Gosson's charge that plays are lies, but implicitly he surrenders into the hands of an elite the authority over this power of constructing what might and should be. Early in the treatise Sidney mystifies the idea of a poet, calling him a Godlike maker with access to a golden world of Platonic ideas (99–101). But in a wonderful instance of the latter end of a tale forgetting its beginning, Sidney's opening, expansive defense of the freedom of the poet as maker leads eventually to his *ex cathedra* imposition of rules of decorum and just imitation within which the freedom of the true poet must be exercised.

Too sophisticated to charge art with being a form of lying, Sidney nonetheless indicts some forms of popular art with being indecorous, crude, unmannerly; in short, of being lower-class, misshapen parodies of elite productions. When Sidney talks of the theater directly, he is quite critical of the imperfect fictions of the popular stage which fail to observe the unities or proper decorum in the separation of kings from clowns, base scurrility from chaste delight (Sidney 1695: 133–7). Good poetry and good poets are thus constructed as quite different from what passes for such in the popular realm. Tellingly, he ends his discussion of the stage thus:

> But I have lavished out too many words of this play matter. I do it because, as they are excelling parts of Poesy, so is there none so much used in England, and none can be more pitifully abused; which, like an unmannerly daughter showing a bad education, causeth her mother Poesy's honesty to be called in question.
>
> (137)

The image draws on popular, and unflattering, stereotypes of the feminine to suggest the dangers surrounding theatrical representation. Poetry, like woman, can be a great good, but the less closely she is guarded – the more popular or "much used" she becomes – the greater the possibility of her dishonesty. Implicitly, aristocratic and masculine control of this precious female commodity is mandated, lest it be debased by popular appropriation. Sidney's defense of poetry, at least when Poesy's dangerous theatrical daughter is concerned, is thus a rather partial affair. His disgruntlement with this "play matter" becomes a site of tension in the text where the aristocrat's uneasiness about the class affiliations of those practicing their craft in and attending the public theater becomes evident.

To sum up: while there are many variations within antitheatrical polemic, the tracts as a whole show the enormous pressure placed on certain ideological positions by changing social conditions and practices, of which the theater becomes a convenient symbol. With varying degrees of passion, these treatises pay homage to a static conception of the social order and an essentialist view of human identity as God-given rather than as forged through participation in social processes. Such views are useful to any social group who feels its privileges (whether old or very newly acquired) threatened by the movements of others. In fact, what seems most troubling about the overt shapeshifting of actors and the elaborate and changing dress of women is that both expose the hollowness of essentialist rhetoric, its antihistorical refusal to acknowledge how changing material conditions

43

in urban London make it possible, and in some cases inevitable, for men and women to assume new social positions and engage in new social practices which make talk of an unchanging social order or a "true" unchanging identity seem either absurd or willfully repressive.

It must be emphasized that the social change which the antitheatrical rhetoric was struggling to manage produced fear and anger and incomprehension in many quarters, not only among the powerful who felt they had something to lose if servants wore velvet or women asserted independence from masculine control of their dress and speech. Agricultural workers displaced from the land by enclosures; retainers who found themselves cut adrift from their positions in great households when their impoverished masters shut up the country estate, gave up "housekeeping," and moved to London: such figures could quite legitimately feel adrift in the world, abandoned into chaos, rather than released into freedom, by the changes around them. These people were *forced* to forge new identities, rather like Edgar in *King Lear* when his social identity was stripped from him by the acts of the ambitious Edmund. The bastard brother embraces the chance to be an actor; the legitimate brother is driven to it unwillingly. And Renaissance drama is full of such displaced types – Bosolas and Vindices and Bussy D'Amboises – who for one reason or another find themselves without a socially defined identity and so are forced to embrace the path of self-fashioning, but with nothing like the enthusiasm of a Pico or the enthusiasm of the gentlemen who people the courtesy books.

In my reading the antitheatrical tracts are a discursive site where the anxiety about social change was both created – by nostalgic narratives of decline and by narratives of adulteration and contamination – and awkwardly managed – by prescriptions about acceptable and unacceptable behaviors and practices. By awkwardly managed I mean simply that the ideological positions taken in the tracts are not necessarily consistent or coherent, as Sidney's position on the theater illustrates. In general, the antitheatricalists were right that in Elizabethan England social relations were changing, that the expanding marketplace had something to do with the changes, and that the professional theater – urban, commercial, and new – was inseparable from the larger ensemble of new institutions and practices permeating the culture. Yet these pamphleteers regularly displaced the faint beginnings of an economic and social analysis with a moral one. They vehemently castigated groups of people for sloth, idleness, and pride when enclosures, internal migration, and the growth of the placeless market often stood behind the behaviors they attributed to weak and sinful natures.

Misrecognitions stud antitheatrical discourse. Often, for example, the writers either do not see or do not admit to the ways they themselves are implicated in the practices they condemn: writing books in which they fashion public personae, often strutting in the borrowed roles of others' learning, and advancing themselves socially by their entrepreneurship as Gosson, for example, seems to have been attempting to do. Largely, also, the antitheatricalists misrecognize the role of the middling sort, the protobourgeoisie, in the social changes they describe (a trait they share, I think, with new historicists).[10] In most antitheatrical tracts the social world is divided between the nobility and the meaner sort who are characterized as lazy, masterless, deceitful, and prone to lechery. Yet it was seldom the poor who spurred the social changes for which they were scapegoated. Rather, it was engrossing landowners, projectors, entrepreneurial merchants, and aspiring London shopkeepers with aspiring wives. Some of the traditional aristocracy were seeking out new forms of wealth, and a fledgling middle class, a protobourgeoisie, was emerging. In fact, the values of thrift, industry, and sobriety promulgated by someone like North-brooke are the values of an emergent class not fully able to recognize itself as such. Ironically, it was in certain plays of the period, such as the works of Dekker and Heywood, that the world view of the middling sort was to receive fuller and more self-conscious articulation. Moreover, members of the London stage companies did not fit exactly within the old categories that divided the world between those who were gentlemen and those who were not. The shareholders of the companies were as much entrepreneurs as servants to an aristocratic master, though the fiction of service was what gave them cultural legitimacy.

Because the theater emerged when England, and especially London, were undergoing rapid social and economic changes, the theater was riddled with contradictions no contemporary commentators could quite grasp. Just as shareholders in the

London companies were both servants to an aristocrat or to the king *and also* enterprising businessmen, so the conditions of production made it possible for theatergoing subjects to be interpellated in competing ways and for a gap to open between the ideological import of the total theatrical experience and the ideological import of the scripts being performed. It is the work of subsequent chapters to explore some of these contradictions and in so doing to build on and to revise the antitheatricalists' picture of the theater as Satan's school and of theatricality as an attribute solely of those who are criminal, sinful, or feminine. I begin, however, by looking at two plays – Dekker's *The Whore of Babylon* and Shakespeare's *Much Ado About Nothing* – that in quite different ways demonstrate how stage plays could share ideological ground with the antitheatricalists.

3

ANTITHEATRICALITY STAGED

The workings of ideology in Dekker's *The Whore of Babylon* and Shakespeare's *Much Ado About Nothing*

How a literary text relates to a context, whether verbal or social, is one of the many issues rethought in the last several decades of literary study. In the past, contextualizing a literary work often meant turning it into an illustration of something assumed to be prior to the text, whether that something were an idea, a political event, or a phenomenon such as social mobility. This reading strategy had several problematic consequences. First, it seemed to suggest that texts had one primary determining context and that textual meaning could be stabilized by aligning a text with its "proper" context. Second, it seemed to suggest that literary texts were always responses to, reflectors of, something prior to and more privileged than themselves by which they could be explained. This denied literature an initiatory role in cultural transformations or social struggles, and it seemed to foreclose the possibility that literature could have an effect on other aspects of the social formation, as well as being altered by them. Third, using literature as illustration of a context invited a flattening of that text, a denial of its plurality and contradictions in favour of a univocal reading of its relation to a particular contextual ground.[1]

I am now going to look at some Renaissance plays that involve the representation of dramatic practices. That I do so following a discussion of the antitheatrical tracts may seem to imply that I view these tracts as providing the context that will explain the plays with which I am concerned. It is not so simple. Plays, tracts, courtesy books – all are informed by a discourse

47

of theatricality that does not by itself exhaust the meaning of any of these texts and is often deployed quite differently in each. I began with the antitheatrical tracts because they are so palpably political and selective in their condemnation of the theater and of theatricality. Even though fissured by contradictions, these are unmistakably partisan documents aimed at intervening in the social struggles of the time. Most early modern plays operated somewhat differently, partly because they were part of an emergent commercial entertainment industry and usually did not announce themselves as having interested stakes in current social conflicts.[2] Consequently, it is not always easy to see that these plays were also implicated in the ideological and material struggles of their moment of production, especially because subsequent literary criticism has often turned them into "timeless" objects above history and ideology. Talking about how playtexts participated in early modern conflicts over the theater and theatricality is complicated, of course, by the fact that the performed plays were *embodiments* of theatricality as well as vehicles for *representing* the theatricality of fictional characters. In this chapter I am primarily going to deal with the representational level of these dramas, with their complex participation in antitheatrical discourse at the level of the dramatic narrative. In the next chapter I will look more closely at the relationship between discourses of theatricality within the plays and the material practices comprising the early modern theatrical event and constituting the early modern subject as theatergoer.

As part of a burgeoning entertainment industry, Renaissance plays gradually, but never totally, separated themselves from the overt didacticism of a homiletic tradition. Of course, enemies of the theater saw it teaching Satan's lessons, and defenders such as Heywood argued that its fictions instilled both morality and patriotism in its spectators. Even the great moralizer, Ben Jonson, had to admit that the marketplace largely determined what shapes his fictions would take; and a playwright such as Shakespeare openly espoused an aesthetic of pleasure-giving, of delivering to audiences what they liked, as they liked it. Feste's refrain, "And we'll strive to please you every day" (*Twelfth Night* V. i. 408), aptly summarizes the first imperative governing play production in the public theater. This hardly meant, however, that plays did not perform the work of ideology: the circulation of constructions of the real which serve particular interests but seem merely to express the natural order of things. As Althusser has convincingly shown, ideology most effectively sutures social subjects into their proper places in the social order when its workings are invisible to those subjects, when, for example, ideology passes as common sense, objective truth, or "mere entertainment" (Althusser 1971: 171–2). In a materialist understanding of the world, in which class and other forms of stratification are preserved in part by means of ideological interpellation, no discourse, not even those we mark as literary, lies outside the domain of the ideological (Bennett 1990: 117–42). Ideology critique, itself never unsituated, examines the interests served by particular textual representations and narratives. It is a double-edged practice – part of a hermeneutics of suspicion, certainly, in that it assumes texts, and reading of texts, serve unannounced and unrecognized political ends; but part, too, of an ameliorative project to interrupt those processes by which privileged cultural narratives are used simply to legitimate the common sense of dominant social groups.

In thinking about the relationship of the early modern public stage to the circulation of ideology within Tudor and Stuart culture, I want to look at two plays, Thomas Dekker's *The Whore of Babylon* and Shakespeare's *Much Ado About Nothing*, in both of which the representation of theatrical practices is a major motif. These plays are interesting to examine in tandem for several reasons. While both to some extent deploy rhetoric and assumptions found in the antitheatrical tracts, they do so in ways that suggest both the potential differences between stage plays and polemical tracts and also the differences between one stage play and another. The meanings and ideological effectivity of antitheatrical discourse depend very much on the context and manner of its deployment.

Dekker's play, probably written in 1606 in the wake of the Gunpowder Plot, is the only one of his works, besides the *Famous History of Sir Thomas Wyatt*, usually classified as a history play (Conover 1969: 112). Heywood in his defense of the stage singled out the history play as a genre particularly suited to the inculcation of patriotism and to the construction, for the people, of a memory of their collective past (Heywood 1612: Book III, F3-F3ᵛ). This view of the history play may in part explain the particular form of Dekker's play which is a highly idealized, nostalgic recreation of events from the reign of Elizabeth I that emphasizes her repulse of Catholic-inspired threats to England's autonomy and to her own safety. The plot focuses on various attempts by the Empress of Rome to infiltrate the court of Elizabeth either to convert her through marriage to the cause of Rome or to murder her if she proves recalcitrant. In the end, the Empress gives up plots of infiltration and launches the Armada. Rearranging chronology and improvising on historical fact, Dekker manages to dramatize or allude to, among other events, the defeat of the Spanish Armada, the alleged plots by Edmund Campion and Dr Lopez on Elizabeth's life, and the plots and executions of Essex and Mary Queen of Scots.

For my purposes, the play holds interest because at one level it is organized by the opposition between theatricality and plainness, the latter implicitly defined as the opposite of deceptive shapeshifting. This opposition is elaborated in many ways. The Empress of Rome, for example, sends operatives to England to do her dirty work and urges them to engage in a variety of self-transformative projects to avoid detection and further their objective of destroying Elizabeth. In the midst of a long catalog of tactics for disguising the self she says: "Or if you walke abroad, be wrapt in clouds,/Have change of haires, of eie-brows, halt with soldiers,/Be shaven and be old women, take all shapes/To escape taking" (III. i. 161–4) (Dekker 1955: 539). A character who represents the King of Spain does just that. At the beginning of the second act he enters, telling his man, dressed as a sailor, to help him adjust his disguise, which at this point is the garb of a grave and learned scholar. He then tells the servant to change out of his own sailor outfit and to get yet another disguise ready for the king to employ later. As he says to his man:

> Stands my beard right? the gowne: I must looke grave,
> White haires like silver cloudes a priviledge have,
> Not to be search'd, or be suspected fowle:
> Make away those two turne coates. Suite me next
> Like to a Sattin divell (bravely), flie
> Your saylers shape: be here immediatly.
> So: excellent: a subtile masque: alls fit:
> This very cap makes my head swell with wit.
>
> (II. ii. 1–8)

He then recounts how, dressed as a soldier, he had previously fomented sedition among poor military men, though now he is turning his attention to the learned classes, in this case to the seduction of a disgruntled scholar named Campeius, a figure for Edmund Campion. At the end of the same scene the king changes clothing yet again:

> To flea off this hypocrisie, tis time,
> Least worne too long, the Foxes skinne be known:
> In our dissembling now we must be brave,
> Make me a courtier: come; Asses I see,
> In nothing but in trappings, different be
> From foote-cloth nags, on which gay fellows ride,
> Save that such gallants gallop in more pride.
>
> (II. ii. 155–61)

Then he persuades a courtier to bury a picture of Elizabeth in the ground with pins like daggers sticking in her heart to cause her to sicken and die.

Lest the spectator miss the implications of all this – i.e. that the minions of the Babylonian Empress will use black magic and any form of Satanic shapeshifting to bolster her counterfeit authority and to seduce disgruntled subjects into sedition – Dekker adds an overtly allegorical layer to his drama featuring the figures of Time, Truth, Falsehood, Double-dealing, and Plaine-dealing. Predictably, Truth, supported by Time the revealer of Truth, resides in Elizabeth's England; Double-dealing and False-hood assist the Empress of Babylon. Plaine-dealing, in my view the only comically rendered character in the play, journeys from Rome to England, switching allegiance from the Empress to Titania when told that in Rome he was seduced by a false apparition of Truth and that the *real* Truth dwells only with Elizabeth. In this regard it is worth noting that one of Elizabeth's mottos, *Semper Eadem*, functioned in part to signal her commitment to an ideology of antitheatrical self-consistency, despite the enormous care which she in actuality lavished on crafting her self-representations.

In obvious ways, the treatment of theatrical shapeshifting in this play recalls the demonizing strategies of the antitheatrical tracts, playing specifically on the associations among disguise, deceit, and Catholicism in Protestant polemic. (Recall, for example, Thomas Tuke's accusation that priests encourage women to paint and to disguise their true natures.) Enemies of England, of the queen, of Protestants – all are emptied of any claim to truthful self-presentation, though in their shiftiness they exercise real power in inciting sedition among the disgruntled members of Elizabeth's polity. Violently anti-Catholic and nationalistic, the play constructs the difference between Prot-estantism and Catholicism, Englishmen and foreigners, chiefly as a difference between an allegiance to essential, unchanging truth and an allegiance to illusion and false appearances.[3] Cer-tainly such images and binarisms would have been familiar in a Protestant culture and would have had special appeal for audience members sympathetic to a critique of James's relative reticence as a Protestant champion (Gasper 1990: 96–102). In short, *The Whore of Babylon* mobilizes an established antitheatri-cal rhetoric overtly to advance a particular political agenda.

Ironically, the play thereby loses some of its ideological force, if by ideology one means, as I do, an interested discourse that passes as universal truth or the common sense of everyone. Repeatedly, as I hope to show, Dekker's play *reveals* the interested nature of its representations. Functioning as a rallying point for political partisans, it does so at the expense of a certain pretense to universality. For example, at the time of its probable composition in 1606, both the play's allegorical elements and its dumbshows (present at the beginning of several acts) would have marked the play as a throwback to an earlier age. Both allegory and dumbshow associate this play with the Elizabethan period: with Elizabeth herself, with an idealized view of her Protestant politics, and with the cultural productions through which she had been honored, such as Spenser's *Fairie Queene*. In short, the play constitutes a form of Elizabethan nostalgia and an implicit critique of James's pacifism. The Gunpowder Plot gave Dekker the opportunity to capitalize on a burst of anti-Catholic sentiment to comment on the contemporary scene through the screen of nostalgia and historical displacement.

It is unclear whether or not Dekker's play was popular. The author wrote in prefatory material to the printed edition that he feared it had been badly mangled by the actors in performance (Dekker 1955: 497–8), which may be a way of justifying an unfavorable audience reaction. It is possible that if this play was not received enthusiastically in 1606, it may have been because, to use modern terms, it too blatantly revealed ideology as ideology, as politically motivated construction, rather than as simple truth, and did so at a place – the site of the stage – where audiences had come to expect their edification and their politics more fully concealed as entertainment. Dekker's anachronistic stagecraft makes the spectator constantly aware of the artifice of what is being enacted, of the scene of representation as just that, a scene of representation, where a very particular and politically motivated construction of reality is being fashioned and disseminated.

In addition, the very requirements of dramatic presentation make Dekker's mobilization of well-worn discourses of deceit and Satanic shapeshifting unpredictably complicated and ambivalent, so that even their overt polemical force is compromised. There is, of course, irony in the fact that a full-scale critique of illusion, shapeshifting, and theatrical practice is enacted by a troupe of professional actors in a theater. While an awareness of this irony does not seem to be registered anywhere in Dekker's text, it could hardly not have been generated in the audience by the fact of the performance context. *The Whore of Babylon* is a highly artificial and "theatrical" play, mirroring in its elaborate spectacles and speaking pageants its characters' preoccupations with artifice and shapeshifting. A gap therefore opens between the play's didactic content and the theatrical mode of production it employs to make its points.

Moreover, in elaborating his allegory of Protestant plainness and Catholic deceit, Dekker employs an implicit debate structure throughout the text, pitting Titania against her opponents in ways probably meant to engender a sense of dramatic conflict, but which ironically end up destabilizing the binary oppositions upon which the play's whole polemical strategy rests. The play opens, for example, with a dumbshow in which Truth and Time, sad and disheveled, awake and rejoice when the hearse of Queen Mary is brought across the stage. Titania then enters with her grave counselors, and Time and Truth present her with a book, presumably the Protestant Bible, which she embraces. Clearly, from an English Protestant perspective, the death of Mary and the crowning of Elizabeth are meant to signal the triumph of truth over the darkness of Satanic idolatry. But the first scene of the play at once underscores the fact that how one interprets these events really is a matter of interpretation. That first scene occurs in the empress's court at Rome where she is raging about

53

the lies spread by Elizabeth's followers concerning her rule. They accuse her churches of being stews, her vestments borrowed, and her glory counterfeit. But, in a counternarrative, she claims it is England where real deceit harbors:

> That strumpet, that inchantresse, (who, in robes
> White as is innocence, and with an eye
> Able to tempt stearne murther to her bed)
> Calles her selfe Truth, has stolne faire Truths attire,
> Her crowne, her sweet songs, counterfets her voyce,
> And by prestigious tricks in sorcerie,
> Ha's raiz'd a base impostor like Truths father:
> This subtile Curtizan sets up againe,
> Whom we but late banisht, to live in caves,
> In rockes and desart mountaines.
>
> (I. i. 56–65)

Clearly two can play at the game of "J'accuse." Having provided a reading of how the English Protestants read her, the Empress reads them in the same terms. Throughout the text each side clings tenaciously to its reading of the other as false counterfeiters. The effect is to call attention to the political motivations underlying such readings, to the malleability of signifiers to the interpretive determinations of various readers.

Plaine-dealing is the figure through whom the difficulties of "proper" interpretation are most comically registered and who ironically does the most to complicate the binary oppositions upon which the text's dominant ideological positions depend. He is clearly a Kent figure, an image of the good counselor who dares to speak truth to power, even when it is dangerous to do so. Having once followed the empress, in England Plaine-dealing becomes an outspoken follower of Titania, roundly criticizing her court, her soldiers, and her realm for their many vices. One recalls the deep satirical thrust of the antitheatrical tracts, their impulse to anatomize *all* the follies of an England given over to Satan and to the theater. But in Dekker's plays such social satire of the contemporary English scene awkwardly contradicts the idealized panegyric of Elizabeth and her rule.[4] While the intent may have been to show Elizabeth as a monarch who can take counsel well and who will work to remove vice from her realm, the effect is to undermine the absolute distinction between her and her Satanic double, the empress. For example, after Plaine-dealing has lambasted Titania's Knights' ward for the drinking, smoking, and gambling he found there, she comments: "You are growne sirra an observer since you came out of Babylon" (II. i. 85–6). He responds:

> Troth mistresse, I left villains and knaves there, and find knaves and fooles here: for your Ordinary is your Isle of Gulles, your ship of fooles, your hospitall of incurable madmen: it is the field where your captaine and brave man is cal'd to the last reckoning, and is overthrown horse and foot: it is the onley schoole to make an honest man a knave: for Intelligencers may heare enough there, to set twenty a begging of lands: it is the strangest Chesse-board in the world.
>
> (II. i. 87–94)

In other words, while the empress and Titania are supposedly moral opposites, their courts are in many ways indistinguishable in terms of the vices they harbor.

Not only does Plaine-dealing see vice in both places, he also has some fairly comic trouble distinguishing Truth from Falsehood. Sent by Titania to dwell with Truth, Plaine-dealing plaintively asks: "But how shall I know, thou art the right truth?" (III. iii. 1). She responds:

> Because I am not painted.
>
> Plain. Nay if thou hast no better coulour then that, ther's no trueth in thee, for Im'e sure your fairest wenches are free of the painters.
>
> Truth. Besides I am not gorgious in attire,
> But simple, plaine and homely; in mine eyes,
> Doves sit, not Sparrowes: on my modest cheekes,
> No witching smiles doe dwell: upon my tongue
> No unchast language lies: my Skins not spotted
> With foule disease, as is that common harlot,
> That baseborne trueth, that lives in Babylon.
>
> Plain. Why? is shee spotted?
>
> Tru. All over, with strange uglines, all over.
> Plain. Then she has got the pox, and lying at my host
> Gryncums, since I left her company: how soever it be thou

55

> and I will live honest togither in one house, because my
> court mistris will have it so: I have beene a Travailer a
> great while, Plaine dealing hath lept from country to
> country, till he had scarece a paire of soales to carrie him.
>
> (III. iii. 2–20)

Truth trots out all the pieties about the plain, unadorned self-evidence of Truth, but if her identity *were* so obvious, Plaine-dealing would not have had to inquire about it. Moreover, his responses suggest that the Empress had not been evidencing any noticeable spots when he left her court. In short, his skepticism corrodes belief in Truth's assertions. Bidden by a new mistress to live with this Truth, he will, but weariness with wandering, more than conviction of Truth's truth, seems to motivate him. His skepticism makes it plain that knowing inner essence from outward signs is nearly impossible, since outward signs, even of plainness, can be assumed like any other disguise.

Of course, I would make no claims that Dekker intended this play to be a demystification of the political functions of an antitheatrical discourse. Certainly in the end he makes Elizabeth and her version of truth triumph over the empress and what is reputed to be her duplicity. This is an unmistakably patriotic, Protestant play in its overt intentions. But neither would I say that the demystifying effects I have been describing are simply the results of my contemporary reading strategies. This play creates what we would now call alienation effects simply by its deployment of devices such as allegory and dumbshow which mark it as old fashioned and propagandistic, especially when the entire work is published in honor of the dead queen. Moreover, in the interests of creating dramatic conflict, Dekker overtly makes truth a battleground over which the Empress and Titania struggle, both accusing the other of "mere counterfeiting." In the process, antitheatrical rhetoric's place as a weapon in political struggle becomes evident. When coupled with Plaine-dealing's corrosive cynicism, the polemical force of the play is threatened. Ironically, in its commitment to the cause of militantly Protestant patriotism, *The Whore of Babylon* uses antitheatrical polemic in a way that diminishes its force by revealing both the interested nature of its deployment and the instability of the binarisms upon which it depends. This play would appeal to a specialized audience of political partisans, but it would not pass as "disinterested" entertainment.

By contrast, Shakespeare's *Much Ado About Nothing*, a play also heavily invested in the representation of dramatic practices, much more effectively performs the essential work of ideology, i.e. the naturalization of interested representations of the real. In particular, it employs antitheatrical discourse in a way that advantages certain social groups without calling attention to that fact. Once one begins to count, one discovers that *Much Ado* is filled with staged shows, inner plays, actors, and interior dramatists. Don Pedro and Don John both devise pageants designed to deceive specific audiences; most of Messina pretends to be someone else at a masked ball at the outset of the play; and the work ends with two shows involving Claudio: in one he plays the role of mourner before an empty tomb he believes contains his betrothed; in the other he plays the groom to a woman – really Hero – whom he believes to be Hero's cousin. I am interested in two things in regard to these aspects of the play: how these representations of theatrical practice function within the Elizabethan context to produce and reproduce class and gender difference within a social order dependent on these differences to justify inequalities of power and privilege, and how modern commentators have depoliticized the play by moralizing it, that is, by focusing on the distinction between good and evil theatricality in the play, thus displacing a political analysis of why particular social groups "naturally" play the opprobrious part in this moral drama.[5]

Reading the play in relationship to the antitheatrical tracts makes its political dimensions more apparent, I think, though Shakespeare's play does not participate in the overtly polemical rantings of those tracts. Far from placing the work "above ideology" however, its distance from overtly polemical intention is what makes it an effective producer and disseminator of ideology, that is, of understandings of relations to the real so effectively naturalized that their constructed and interested character is obscured. Consequently, much more than is true with *The Whore of Babylon*, the ideological work performed by the discourse of theatricality in this play has to be unearthed through the work of ideology critique, through a strategy of reading aimed at speaking the unspoken of the text and at pressuring its contradictions to reveal its mediations of social struggle.

In regard to its representations of theatricality, one might expect *Much Ado* to be unequivocally positive. After all, the work itself is a play. But, just as support for the theatricality of *certain* groups can be found in the antitheatrical tracts, making them speak, as it were, against themselves, so Shakespeare's play speaks against itself in several important senses. Although *Much Ado* is a play, and although it dramatizes a world permeated with theatrical practices, it also eventually leaves "the better sort" in charge of theatrical practices and disciplines upstarts who would illegitimately seize such power. Read in relationship to the antitheatrical tracts, the play thus appears to police its own pro-theater tendencies by acknowledging the validity of much antitheatrical polemic and reproducing its writing of the social order, especially its fear of the dangerous duplicity of women and of those who aspire beyond their station.

And yet, even as it enacts the disciplining of upstarts and the policing of theatrical power advocated by the antitheatrical tracts, the play as a material phenomenon – as produced on the Elizabethan public stage, rather than a modern one – literally involved men of low estate assuming the garments of women, playing the parts of kings and aristocrats, and gaining economic power from the sale of dramatic illusions. This is a case where the ideological function of the dramatic narrative comes into clear, if unacknowledged, conflict with the ideological implications of the material conditions of Elizabethan theater production. Moreover, the play also speaks against itself in regard to its presentation of the relationship between truth and illusion. While it circulates the idea that in some absolute sense a true reading of the world is possible, a reading which eludes the "distortions" and mediations of dramatic illusion, that view is countered by the dramatization of a world in which truth is discursively produced and authorized and so remains unknowable outside a set of practices, including theatrical practices, which secure one understanding of the world at the expense of another.[6] To tease out these contradictions and to consider their ideological implications is the purpose of what follows.

At its center *Much Ado* seems to dramatize the social consequences of staging lies. Don John precipitates the play's crisis by having a servant, Margaret, impersonate her mistress, Hero, in a love encounter observed by Hero's husband-to-be and Don John's brother. These theatrics make Hero appear a whore and lead directly to her denunciation in the church. This deception is clearly coded as evil: it is engineered by a bastard, involves the transgressive act of a servant wearing the clothes of one of higher rank, and leads to the threat of death for several of the play's characters.

Before discussing this evil trick further, however, I want to note the changes Shakespeare made in his source material which radically compounded the amount of theatricality in the play as a whole. For example, while all the sources contain the trick at the window, none contains the Benedick and Beatrice subplot which depends on Don Pedro's theatrical deceptions of each of them (Prouty 1950: 1). Moreover, while the source stories have two men, usually friends, vying for the Hero figure (Prouty 1950: 34), Shakespeare substitutes, instead, a rivalry between Don Pedro and his bastard brother – not for actual possession of the woman – but for power, though the control of women is a chief way of establishing masculine power in the play. This rivalry is largely carried on through competing theatrical tricks. If Don Pedro, the seeming agent for comic union, uses theatrical deception to promote marriages, Don John uses it to thwart his brother's fictions and to contest his brother's power.

The result of these changes is a series of highly overdetermined theatrical situations which betray a deeply conflictual psychic-social zone. None of the play's impersonations and playlets is unproblematical. When Don Pedro impersonates Claudio at the masked ball, for example, he doesn't unproblematically further Claudio's desires. Instead, his action opens the door for Don John's meddling and for a number of "mistakings." Moreover, even Don Pedro, the initiator of so much of the play's disguise and theatrical cozenage, cannot see through the pageant staged at Hero's window.

In trying to make sense of the play's treatment of theatricality, twentieth-century humanist criticism has typically made two moves: one involves drawing clear moral distinctions between "good" and "bad" theatrical practices; the other involves reassuring readers that the play offers ways to cope with – to see through – omnipresent theatrical deception. Richard Henze typifies the dominant critical position in discriminating between one form of theatrical deception which "leads to social peace, to marriage, to the end of deceit" and another which "breeds conflict and distrust and leads even Beatrice to desire the heart of Claudio in the marketplace" (1971: 188). Later I will examine the implicit assumptions lying behind the disappointed phrase, "even Beatrice," but for the moment I wish simply to point out that most readings of the play use the two brothers to figure good and evil theatricality. Indeed, most readings of the play depend, crucially, on maintaining differences in the motives of the two men and in the social consequences of their practices. Similarly, many readings insist on Shakespeare's insistence that beneath the world of unstable appearances there is a world of essences to which man has access if he has, paradoxically, either faith or careful noting skills. Those possessing faith, an essentially mystified notion encompassing both intuition and religious belief, can comprehend the truth which can't be seen, but which lies behind the distortions produced by deceivers. Thus Beatrice sees beyond the appearance of Hero's guilt; and Dogberry and Verges, God's naturals, intuitively know a thief despite misunderstanding utterly his actual language. On the other hand, illusion can also be pierced by careful noting, a pragmatic and practical skill, one paradoxically more congruent with the dawning scientific age than the waning age of faith. Thus the Friar is said to take careful note of Hero in the church and by her blushes and behavior is able to pierce the lies of Don John's fictions. Henze, again, presents a characteristic summation of the dominant critical position: "This combination of intuitive trust and careful observation seems to be the one that the play recommends" (1971: 194). I wish to challenge the focus of this criticism, first by substituting a political and social for a moral analysis of the play's theatrical practices and, second, by looking, not at how the individual subject can discern truth, but at the role of authority and authoritative discourses in delimiting what can be recognized as true.

It is easy to provide a moral reading of Don John. He is the play's designated villian, its exemplification of the evil dramatist; and his chief deception – the substitution of Margaret for Hero at the bedroom window – is clearly a malicious act. Yet a characterological focus on Don John as origin of evil can obscure the extent to which the assumptions about women upon which his trick depends are shared by other men in the play. The trick at the window silently assumes and further circulates the idea that women are universally prone to deception and impersonation. This is a cultural construction of the feminine, familiar from the antitheatrical tracts, which serves the political end of justifying men's control and repression of the volatile and duplicitous female. Don John depends on the currency of this construction of woman in Messina, and he is not disappointed. Faced with Don John's accusations, many men – including Hero's father – quickly conclude she has merely been impersonating virtue (Berger 1982: 306–7). In short, Don John lies about Hero, but his lie works because it easily passes in Messina as a truthful reading of women.

Second, while Don John is the play's villain, he is also the bastard brother of the play's highest-ranking figure. This fact is ideologically significant because it locates the "natural" origins of social disruption in those who do not legitimately occupy a place in the traditional social order. Certainly, in the ideological economy of the play it is useful that the dangerous and threatening aspects of theatricality be located in and exorcised by the punishment of a scapegoat figure. While many figures *within* the play make Hero the scapegoat for their fears, for the audience the scapegoat is Don John, illegitimate intruder among the ranks of the aristocracy. Thus, much as in the antitheatrical tracts, women and "bastards" (those who have no legitimate social position or have forsaken that position) are figured as the natural and inevitable source of social disruption and evil. Moreover, the very fact that Don John is a bastard further implicates women in crime. As Harry Berger writes: "The play's two scapegoats are a bastard named Trouble and a woman named Hero, and his bastardy tells us where the blame lies: like Edmund, no doubt, he is a testimony both to his father's prowess and to his mother's sin – a by-product of the frailty named Woman" (1982: 311).

Thus Don John is both a testimony to woman's weakness and a social outsider, someone tolerated within Messinian society only on the say-so of his legitimate brother. He is, moreover, punished for usurping an activity – the manipulation of the world through theatrical fictions – which is from first to last in this play associated with aristocratic male privilege. While women are characterized as deceivers, literally, as Balthasar's song more accurately declares, it is "men [who] were deceivers ever" (II. iii. 63), especially men in power.[7] Don Pedro is, after all, the play's chief dissembler. It is he who first employs theatrical deception in his plan to woo Hero for Claudio, and he who then goes on to arrange the playlets by which Benedick and Beatrice are made to fall in love. When Claudio first approaches Don Pedro about marrying Hero, for example, the Prince volunteers in his own person to negotiate the contract between his retainer and his old friend's daughter. Moreover, while the Hero figure in the sources is of humble origins, this is not true of Shakespeare's Hero (Prouty 1950: 43–4). Don Pedro is thus not in the ambiguous position of sanctioning a marriage across class lines, but instead promotes a union between social equals and so strengthens the existing social order.

His actions in regard to Benedick and Beatrice are more complex, and I will discuss them further below, but what they achieve is the disciplining of social renegades and their submission to the authority of Don Pedro and to the institution of marriage which it seems his special function to promote. Benedick, of course, openly scoffs at marriage throughout a good portion of the play; and Beatrice turns aside a marriage proposal – however seriously meant – from Don Pedro himself. Through his staged pageants, Don Pedro asserts control over these two renegades and checks the socially subversive impulse their refusal to marry implies. What Don John by his deceptions thus usurps is the prerogative of theatrical deception by which his legitimate brother controls Messina. If Don Pedro is the one first to make use of impersonation and theatrical tricks, Don John is the copycat who imitates the initial trick at the bedroom window. If Don Pedro exercises power by arranging marriages, Don John counters that power by spoiling marriages and does so using the very tools of theatrical deception employed by Don Pedro. The bastard's acts thus appropriate a power the play seeks to lodge with the legitimate brother. At play's end, it is this aggression for which the worst punishment is promised.

Further, the very *way* the various deceptions of the two brothers are materially represented on the stage has specific ideological consequences. Don John's crucial deception is his substitution of maid for mistress at the bedroom window. This trick involves a transgression against hierarchy in which, as on the public stage itself, an inferior assumes the borrowed robes of a social superior. This action is not dramatized. Consigned to the realm of the "unseen," its consequences disappear utterly – like a bad dream – at play's end. By contrast, Don Pedro's two most elaborate deceptions, the playlets put on for Benedick and Beatrice, *are* dramatized and are presented as part of the prerogatives of Messina's highest-ranking visitor. Ironically, these presentational choices naturalize Don Pedro's practice so that, as in all ideological effects, the arbitrary passes as the inevitable. Moreover, the theater audience, knowing of Don Pedro's plans and taking pleasure in the spectacle of Benedick and Beatrice's recantation of prior positions, is fully complicit with Don Pedro's trick, legitimating it by laughter. By contrast, the bastard's acts are represented as evil and as so outside the natural order that they are assigned to the unreality of the unseen. There is no opportunity for audience involvement in the unfolding of his plot. What results is the production of differences between similar activities in ways that obscure the social differences justified and held in place by moral categories. As in the theatrical tracts, a key question turns out to be: whose fiction-making activities are to be construed as legitimate? And, as in those tracts, the answer involves matters of gender and rank as much as moral motive. Much modern criticism of the play, by focusing so resolutely on the morality of deception, has been complicit in allowing to pass unnoted the function of moral categories in reproducing existing power relations and social arrangements.

This criticism has also been obsessed with the problem of how we can "see through" the play's many theatrical practices to a truth not obscured by lies. This play, more than most, seems to engender in readers fears about never getting to "the real," but of being trapped in competing and manipulative discursive constructions of it. Focusing on getting outside of discourse, through either the empiricism of careful noting or the transcendentalism of faith, shortcircuits a political analysis of how truth effects are produced through discourse, and of the social origins of those dissenting perspectives through which "truth" is exposed as somebody's truth.

The utopian nature of the desire to escape discourse is perhaps best seen by looking at the play's handling of Dogberry and Verges who, with their apparently intuitive recognition of villainy, are crucial to any reading which insists on the ultimate transparency of the world to the faithful and/or the astute. First of all, there is something improbable about their rescue of Messina from illusion. For three-quarters of the play illusions seem impermeable. Don Pedro and Claudio fall victim to them as do the witty and skeptical Beatrice and Benedick. The world is only righted by two lower-class figures who flounder mightily in the Queen's English, and who capture the villains virtually by instinct rather than by any rational understanding of what was overheard or said or done by anyone. Moreover, it seems that the gift of intuition is bought at the price of speech and rationality. Dogberry and Verges exist almost outside of language, and this placement denies them any real social power. Constructed as God's naturals, these lower-class figures conveniently solve society's problems without ever threatening its central values or power relations or providing an alternative understanding of the social order (Kreiger 1979: 61). Pathetically eager to please their betters, they are obsessively preoccupied with that phantom, Deformed, whose chief crime, besides thievery, seems to be that he "goes up and down like a gentleman" (III. iii. 126–7) and spends money beyond his ability or desire to repay it (V. i. 308–12). Dogberry and Verges are as concerned as their betters to discipline upstarts. Unlike the more rebellious, clever, and even dangerous lower-class figures in some of Shakespeare's plays – Pompey, Jack Cade, Feste, Pistol – Dogberry and Verges perform a sentimental, utopian function. They keep alive the dream of a world where good and evil are transparent to the eye of innocence and inferiors correct the "mistakings" of their betters without ever threatening the essential beliefs of those betters.

The utopian impulse simply to escape the world of deception and mediation not only finds its logical end in the garbled speech of Dogberry and Verges, but is also strongly countered by other aspects of the play's action which point to the conclusion that in a thoroughly dramatistic universe one can escape neither from discourse nor from the play of power which authorizes the truth of one construction of the world over another. In Elizabethan culture and in this play, a chief form of power is, of course, theatrical power. The role of theatrical fictions as instruments of power and as a means of compelling belief in a particular view of truth is most graphically shown in Don Pedro's successful manipulation of Benedick and Beatrice. Readers often point out that these two are depicted as showing a keen interest in one another from the play's opening moments and as, perhaps, having once been romantically involved. By contrast, I want to focus on the role of Don Pedro's pageants in producing their love. While a modern discourse of love understands it as, essentially, a private, inwardly produced emotion which serves as the motive for marriage, in the Renaissance many upper-class marriages had other motives, political, economic, or social. In *Much Ado*, through the actions of Don Pedro one can see the investment of established authority in using marriage to reproduce existing social relations (both gender and class relations) and to control threats to the social order. Far from *discovering* Benedick's and Beatrice's pre-existent love, Don Pedro works hard to *create* it. When the two of them "fall in love," they do not so much obey a spontaneous, privately engendered emotion as reveal their successful interpellation into particular positions within a gendered social order.[8] In this play, Don Pedro is the agent of such interpellation. He never indicates that he sees a repressed attraction between Benedick and Beatrice, nor does he present his fictions as simply revealing that truth. Instead, his object is to create love where its existence seems impossible and thus to control the social world around him. He places both Benedick and Beatrice as subjects of a love discourse in which a role for each to play is clearly marked, the role of "the normal" male and female.

The two playlets, however, though having the same general aim of making social renegades conform, also produce gender difference in the process. To be a "normal" male is not the same as being a "normal" female. In discussing Beatrice before Benedick, Leonato and his friends construct her as a vulnerable, pitiful victim. Her tears, her sleeplessness, her indecision – all are dwelt on in loving detail. The role mapped for Benedick is to be her rescuer, to become more "manly" by accepting his duty to succor women as well as to fight wars. And Benedick takes up his assigned place in the gendered social order by vowing to put aside his pride and accept her love. He presents his change of heart as a species of "growing up." As he says, "A man loves the meat in his youth that he cannot endure in his age" (II. iii. 238–40), and the misogyny he had embraced is an example of such meat now displaced by the maturer pleasure of peopling the world and receiving a woman's adoration. By contrast, the conversation staged for Beatrice only briefly focuses on Benedick's suffering. He is presented as the good man any woman would be a fool to scorn, but most of the attention focuses on how unnatural her pride, her wit, and her independence are. Her great sin is to be "so odd, and from all fashions" (III. i. 72), that is, so quick in mocking men who are to be revered, not exposed to ridicule. Tellingly, Beatrice shows her successful interpellation into the gendered social order by vowing to tame her "wild heart" to Benedick's "loving hand" (III. i. 112) – like a bird or an animal being domesticated. He becomes the protector and tamer, and she the tamed repentant. And while Beatrice's character continues to show traces of the merry-shrew schema which served as Shakespeare's basic model, the two interior plays decisively mark the turn in the subplot toward marriage and the partial righting of the social order by the interpellation of social renegades into gendered and socially less iconoclastic subject positions.

The whole feat constitutes a remarkable display of power on Don Pedro's part. Using theatrical means, he offers Benedick and Beatrice understandings of self and other that serve his own ends. That Benedick and Beatrice accept his fictions as truth depends on a number of factors, including the authority of those promulgating this vision of truth. Benedick and Beatrice believe the lies being voiced in the two eavesdropping encounters first because it is their friends who speak these lies. And while the cynical Benedick can imagine his friends as deceivers, he cannot think this of the grave Leonato. "I should think this a gull, but that the white-bearded fellow speaks it. Knavery cannot sure hide himself in such reverence" (II. iii. 118–20). Age has authorizing force. Further, Don Pedro's constructions are taken as true because they have the authority of cultural stereotypes. He writes Benedick and Beatrice for one another in terms that resonate, as I have argued, with cultural definitions of "man-in-love" and "woman-in-love." Similarly, Don Pedro and Claudio believe the deception at Hero's window, not only because they trust the testimony of their eyes, but also because what Don John tells them has the truth of stereotype as well. Hero is the whore whose appetites are disguised by the illusion of virtue. Moreover, once Don Pedro and Claudio doubt Hero, it is their authority which plays a large part in making Leonato doubt his own daughter in the church. Those further down the social scale have less legitimating power. When in I. ii Antonio tells Leonato that a serving man has heard the Prince say he wants to marry Hero, Leonato asks at once: "Hath the fellow any wit that told you this?" When Antonio replies "A good sharp fellow" (I. ii. 17–18), Leonato still decides to "hold it [the report] as a dream till it appear itself" (20–1). Nothing causes such skepticism in a play in which everyone is remarkably credulous so much as the lowly social status of the reporter.

Consequently, although critics have been quick to deny that theatrical fictions create Benedick and Beatrice's love, the work can be read otherwise as encoding the process by which the powerful determine truth, and revealing the way belief depends upon a fiction's congruence with the common sense of culture. Told by several people that Don Pedro wooed Hero for himself, Claudio responds: "Tis certain so, the Prince woos for himself./Friendship is constant in all other things/Save in the office and affairs of love" (II. i. 174–6). This truism makes it easy to believe the truth of a particular tale of violated friendship. The more a fiction draws on conventional schemata, the more it appears true to life.

In such a context the play reveals how hard it is for marginal figures to counter common sense or to overturn the constructions of the powerful, though social marginality is more likely than either careful noting or faith to be the cause of one's ability to see the arbitrary nature of power's truths. In this play, women are clearly marginal to the male order. When Hero hears herself named whore at her wedding, she does not contest that construction of herself; she swoons beneath its weight. It is as if there were no voice with which to protest the forces inscribing her within the order of "fallen" women. Even the Friar, another figure marginal to the real power in Messina, cannot directly contest the stories endorsed by Don Pedro. He must work by indirection, knowing all the while that his fictions may not alter the fixed views of Claudio and Don Pedro and that Hero may live out her life in a convent. In this context, when existing authority so clearly predetermines what will count as truth, the use of the powerless Dogberry and Verges to rescue the world seems all the more a kind of wish fulfillment or magical thinking: an attempt to reconcile the recognition of power's power to determine the truth with a worldview in which truth stands outside its discursive production in a social field.

Beatrice's role in the church is more complex. Drawn to the pattern of the witty shrew, Beatrice for much of the play does not see the world as others see it. Early in the play she is depicted as resisting the patriarchal dictum that the natural destiny of all women is marriage; similarly, her response to the revelations about Hero reveals she does not accept the misogynist dictum that all women are whores. It is precisely Beatrice's iconoclasm that Don Pedro's playlet seems designed to contain. Iconoclastic voices such as hers need to be recuperated or silenced. In the church, however, no recuperation of her position seems possible. She refuses Don John's assimilation of Hero to the stereotype of whore, but she cannot by her voice triumph over Don Pedro's authority. This, of course, is why she is driven to demand that Benedick "kill Claudio" (IV. i. 289), a statement which has led to her denunciation in a good deal of criticism (recall Henze's "even Beatrice" which, by implicitly constructing women as peacemakers and repositories of good sense, writes their anger as more transgressive than men's), but which can be read as an acknowledgment that in a world where power resides in the words of powerful men, the violence their speaking can do can be successfully countered – not by the speaking of women – but by the literal violence of the sword.

Of course, at this juncture another ideological fissure opens in the play. When Benedick and Beatrice are depicted as standing out against marriage, they figure a challenge to the social order. When led to confess love for one another, they take up their places within that gendered order. But pretty clearly for Don Pedro their doing so was not supposed to threaten the patriarchal system. The wife was to be the tamed bird, submissive to her husband's hand, and the bonds between men were not seriously to be disturbed, as we see in Claudio's offer to marry and then promptly to escort Don Pedro on the next stages of his journey. He may be about to become a husband, but that seems not to disturb the primacy of his role as attendant upon the Duke. But, ironically, the bond with a woman *does* disrupt Benedick's bonds to men. The subject position of "lover" into which Don Pedro was so eager to maneuver his friend comes into conflict with the claims of male friendship, producing disequilibrium in the social order. At first, Benedick as lover offered no threat to Don Pedro. His perfume, his shaving, his seeking out of Beatrice's picture – all his actions reveal him very much the stereotypical and somewhat comic lover. He is exhibiting the appropriate masculine behavior Don Pedro and Claudio both intended to elicit and undergoing a rite of passage which marks him as "of the company of men" in a new way. Beatrice's "Kill Claudio," however, forces the issue of competing loyalties, revealing the potential contradictions in Benedick's position. And when Benedick is depicted as choosing faith in Beatrice over loyalty to Claudio and Don Pedro, these former friends are at first simply incredulous. They cannot credit this disruption of the patriarchal order.

The ending of the play "takes care" of this problem. As is the case with many of Shakespeare's comedies, the ending of *Much Ado* has a strongly recuperative function as it attempts to smooth over the contradictions or fissures that have opened in the course of the play. In several obvious ways the ending seems to affirm the "naturalness" of a hierarchical, male-dominated social order and to treat challenges to that order, and to the privileges of its beneficiaries, as mere illusions or temporary aberrations. For example, the tension between male–male and male–female bonds simply disappears with Borachio's confession. There is no duel, and in the final scene the renewed friendship of Claudio and Benedick, affirmed by the exchange of cuckold jokes, is as prominent as their simultaneous marriages. In addition, the transgressive appropriation of theatrical power by the bastard Don John collapses with equal suddenness. He is, as we learn by report, captured and held for punishment, but he is allowed no moment on the stage, a fact once more contributing to our sense that the threat he poses has no ultimate reality.

Less obvious, but equally necessary to a conservative righting of the social order, is the process by which Act V of *Much Ado* relegitimates theatricality as a vehicle for the exercise, by aristocratic males, of power. When Don Pedro became the credulous audience to his brother's fictions, it is as though – in the play's economy of power – he loses the ability to control the world of Messina. Not only Benedick and Beatrice, but Antonio and Leonato, as well, slide outside his control. Violence threatens on several fronts, and the Friar's feeble fictions affect very little. Even with Borachio's confession, no marriages occur. It is as if the world of Messina cannot be "well" until the power of fiction making has been relodged with duly constituted authority. This occurs when the patriarch, Leonato, takes up the task of righting the social order through a series of fictions to be enacted at Hero's tomb and at a second wedding. Hero, having died for the imagined crime of the independent use of her sexuality, is reborn when rewritten as the chaste servant of male desire. While it is often argued that through the second wedding Claudio is being taught to have faith in womankind, despite appearances (Dennis 1973: 231–5), I read the wedding as a lesson in having faith in the authority of social superiors, a lesson to which Claudio is already predisposed. He has always been ready to take Don Pedro's advice, especially about love (Berry 1972: 169), and the gift of Hero at play's end implies simply that rewards will continue to flow from such obedience. What he gets is the still-silent Hero, the blank sheet upon which men write whore or goddess as their fears or desires dictate.[9] The figure of the compliant woman becomes the instrument through which men (Claudio, Don Pedro, Antonio, and Leonato) reconcile their differences.

But while Hero is regranted the status of goddess, the antifeminism which caused her original denigration surfaces again in the horn jokes that figure so prominently in the play's final moments. "There is no staff more reverent than one tipped with horn" (V. iv. 123–4). As the antitheatrical tracts insist, women are duplicitous; they marry men to make them cuckolds. Admittedly, Claudio also says Benedick may prove a "double dealer," (V. iv. 114), but from line 44, when Claudio first mentions Benedick's fear of horns tipped with gold, the scene returns again and again to the threat men face in entrusting their honor to women in marriage. At the same time that the play quietly revalorizes the exercise of theatrical power by aristocratic males, it continues to locate – now less in bastards, but still in women – the threat of a dangerous and unsanctioned theatricality. Moreover, while Beatrice is not "silenced" at the end of the scene, she is emphatically less in charge than in earlier scenes, and her mouth is finally stopped with Benedick's kiss. Thereafter it is he who dominates the dialogue and proposes the dance with which to "lighten" the men's hearts before they marry, as if the prospect is one which has made those hearts heavy.

A final word about the scene and its legitimation of aristocratic, male theatricality. Crucial to this project, as I see it, is the erasure of any lingering suspicion that the fictions of a Don Pedro or a Leonato tamper with nature, rather than express it more fully. Only then can dramatistic and essentialist views of the world be held in tenuous reconciliation. In fact, the final moments of the play can be read as advancing the proposition that, while illusion is everywhere, good fictions merely reveal a pre-existent truth of nature (Beatrice's and Benedick's love, Hero's chastity), while evil fictions (Hero's promiscuity) which distort nature melt like manna in the sun and their perpetrators disappear. Consequently, Benedick and Beatrice must both learn of Don Pedro's tricks and also affirm, willingly and freely, the reality of their love for one another. At first they demur. What leads to their capitulation is the production of love sonnets each has written. What their hands have penned, their hearts must have engendered. And yet, of course, the sonnet form in the 1590s was the most highly conventional genre imaginable. In it one finds already written the text of love. Having been constructed by Don Pedro as lovers, Benedick and Beatrice *must* write sonnets, their production attesting less to the pre-existence of their love than to their successful interpellation into a gendered social order. And yet, by happy sleight of hand, what is their *destiny* within that order is made to seem their *choice*. This maneuver affords another instance of inter-class accommodation as the aristocratic ideology of arranged property marriages is made to appear seamlessly compatible with emergent middle-class ideologies of love and individual choice as preconditions for marital union.

Shakespeare's romantic comedies often provide such utopian resolutions to the strains and contradictions of the period. The comic form, however, was not to serve Shakespeare, or, more properly, his culture, much longer in the form apparent in the high or romantic comedies. In 1604, in writing *Measure for Measure*, he creates a comic authority figure, the Duke, who increasingly uses the arts of theater to order a disordered society. Yet in the end no one is convinced that the Duke's visions merely reveal a pre-existing social reality. (Does Angelo love Mariana and just not know it?) The ending of that play makes much clearer than does *Much Ado* that when power's fictions fail to be persuasive, coercion will enforce their truth. Eventually, in a play like *Lear*, the potential moral bankruptcy of authority and its power to compel – if not belief – at least compliance, are openly acknowledged: "a dog's obey'd in office" (IV. vi. 158–9).

Much Ado hints at these things, but only obliquely. It polices its positive depiction of omnipresent theatrical practices by creating a villainous and illegitimate fiction maker who simply

71

tells lies. The play thus seems irreproachably conservative in its insistence that the power of theatrical illusion-mongering belongs in the hands of the better sort and that their fictions simply reproduce the truths of nature. And yet, as I have argued, the play differs from itself in ways that allow other readings – readings which reveal the constitutive, as opposed to the reflective, power of discursive practices, including theatrical practices, and the role of authority, not nature, in securing the precedence of one truth over other possible truths. Moreover, under the pressure of a political analysis, the play's production of heroes and villains becomes visible as a strategy for holding in place certain inequalities of power and privilege.

But in approaching the self-divisions and contradictions of this work, the contemporary critic has in one respect less access to these features of the play than did the Elizabethan theatergoer. We watch *Much Ado* within institutions which are citadels of high culture and which by and large employ middle-class actors of both sexes. People sitting in the new and culturally contested institution of the Elizabethan public theater on the one hand watched a fiction in which the theatrical practices of a bastard and a woman wearing her mistress's clothes were roundly castigated, even while on the other the agents of representation were most certainly men of mean estate who for their own profit assumed the clothes of women and of noblemen on the stage. As Robert Weimann has argued, a potential contradiction exists between what is being represented and who is doing the representing and under what material conditions (Weimann 1987: 268). For all its affinities with the antitheatrical tracts, *Much Ado* simply because it *is* a stage play, cannot occupy the same cultural space or produce exactly the same ideological effects as these tracts. In the next chapter I want to focus precisely on the scene of representation in the playhouse both to define more fully how the theater could alter the ideological import of discourses it shared with other sites in culture and to examine the political consequences of playgoing for particular categories of Renaissance subjects, especially women.

4

THE MATERIALITY OF IDEOLOGY

Women as spectators, spectacles, and paying customers in the English public theater

In dealing with *The Whore of Babylon* and *Much Ado About Nothing* I have focused primarily on the representational level of each play and on the political implications of how each depicts particular kinds of theatrical practice. But, of course, as I suggested at the end of the last chapter, theater involves a very particular scene of representation, and that scene not only affects the ideological import of the narratives enacted on the stage; it also creates the possibility of a politics of the playhouse as a supplement and/or alternative to the politics of the play-script. In the Renaissance public amphitheaters playgoing involved much more than being the witness to an enacted narra-tive. It also involved paying money to enter the playhouse, and it involved mingling with, observing, and being observed by playgoers of at least two sexes and several social classes. The political implications of these interactions and activities clearly worried enemies of the theater as much as did the possible seditious or lascivious nature of the representations enacted on the stage proper. And I am going to argue that the antitheatri-calists were in this instance onto something. For some subjects, playgoing itself could be as disruptive of established social relations as watching the most iconoclastic drama.

To begin to tease out what is involved in a politics of Renais-sance playgoing for different Elizabethan subjects, especially women, I want to begin by looking at a text included in the "Documents of Control" section of E. K. Chambers' *The Eliza-bethan Stage*, a 1574 Act of the Common Council of London which attempts to restrain and regulate public playing within the Liberties. The reasons given for such restraint are numerous and familiar: the gathering together of playgoers in inns and yards spreads the plague; it creates opportunities for illicit sexual encounters; and it provides the occasion for the dissemination, from the stage, of "unchaste, uncomelye, and unshamefaste speeches and doynges" (Chambers 1923: 273–4). The document is long, and it contains little that would surprise anyone familiar with Renaissance antitheatrical polemic or with the numerous petitions sent by the City to the queen and her council urging the restraint of playing during the next thirty years. Particularly interesting, however, is the way the document concludes:

> this Acte (otherwise than towchinge the publishinge of unchaste, sedycious, and unmete matters:) shall not extend to anie plaies, Enterludes, Comodies, Tragidies, or shewes to be played or shewed in the pryvate hous, dwellinge, or lodginge of anie nobleman, Citizen, or gentleman, which shall or will then have the same thear so played or shewed in his presence for the festyvitie of anie marriage, Assemblye of ffrendes, or otherlyke cawse withowte publique or Commen Collection of money of the Auditorie or behoulders theareof, reservinge alwaie to the Lorde Maior and Aldermen for the tyme beinge the Judgement and construction Accordinge to equitie what shalbe Counted suche a playenge or shewing in a pryvate place, anie things in this Acte to the Contrarie notwithstanding.
>
> (Chambers 1923: 276)

What is striking to me here is the absolutely clear demarcation between the dangers of public playing, involving the "Commen Collection of money of the Auditorie," and the acceptability of playing within a "pryvate hous, dwellinge, or lodginge" where presumably no money was collected and where the audience had therefore not been transformed by a commercial transaction from guests to customers. As was to be true in a number of antitheatrical tracts and petitions from the city, what is specified here as objectionable about certain kinds of theatrical activity is less the matter or content of plays *per se*, and more the practices surrounding public playing: specifically, the removal of the scene of playing from the controlled space of the nobleman's house to a public venue; the dailiness of public playing versus its occasional use, for example, as part of a wedding festivity; the transformation of those who attend the play from guests or clients of a great man or wealthy citizen to paying customers; and, implicitly, the transformation of dramatists from straightforward servants of the nobility to something more akin to artisan entrepreneurs. In short, in this document public playing is presented as altering social relations by the emergent material practices attendant upon play production and attendance, quite apart from any consideration of the ideological import of the fictions enacted on the stage.

Another document written a few years later, when amphitheater playhouses were an established fact, underscores a similar point. In *The Schoole of Abuse*, 1579, Stephen Gosson, drawing on Ovid and classical attacks on the theater, rehearses a number of objections to the public theater that, as we have seen, became standard tropes of English antitheatrical polemic: theater teaches immorality; it allures the senses rather than improves the mind; it encourages flouting of the sumptuary laws; it serves as a meeting place for whores and their customers. While Gosson certainly raises objections to the *content* of plays, he too is keenly alert to the disruptive potential embedded in the very activity of going to a play. It provides occasion, for example, for the conspicuous display of ornate attire and for the promiscuous mixing together of social groups. The money that allowed an upstart crow to ape the clothes of his betters and to display them at the theater also allowed him to purchase a seat in the galleries. While the public theaters were hierarchically designed to reflect older status categories (common men in the pit; gentlemen in the galleries; lords on the very top), in actuality one's place at the public theater was determined less by one's rank than by one's ability or willingness to pay for choice or less choice places. Money thus stratified the audience in ways at least potentially at odds with older modes of stratification, a fact with which Ben Jonson was still ruefully coming to terms several decades later when in the preface to *Bartholomew Fair* he satirically enjoined various members of the audience at the Hope Theatre to offer criticism of his play strictly in proportion to the amount of money they had laid out at the theater door.

It is further agreed that every person here have his or their free-will of censure, to like or dislike at their own charge, the author having now departed with his right: it shall be lawful for any man to judge his six pen'orth, his twelve pen'orth, so to his eighteen pence, two shillings, half a crown, to the value of his place; provided always his place get not above his wit. And if he pay for half a dozen, he may censure for all them too, so that he will undertake that they shall be silent. He shall put in for censures here as they do for lots at the lottery; marry, if he drop but sixpence at the door, and will censure a crown's worth, it is thought there is no conscience or justice in that.

(Jonson 1963: 30–1; Induction, ll. 76–86)

At court, as Jonson's epilogue to the same play suggests, he can count on a spectator, the king, whose judgments are absolute and whose position is fixed, unaffected by the fluidity of market relations. In the public theater things are different. Much to Jonson's dismay, his art has become rather too much like a Bartholomew Fair commodity liable to judgment by those who can and will pay to see it, whatever their rank, education, and taste.

I wish to suggest that in such a context the ideological consequences of playgoing might be quite different for different social groups. Gosson indirectly broaches this issue in what is for me the most interesting part of his tract, namely, the concluding epistle, which is addressed to "the Gentlewomen Citizens of London," a category of playgoer apparently significant enough to warrant Gosson's specific attention.[1] From Andrew Gurr's important study, *Playgoing in Shakespeare's London*, we know that women were in the public theater in significant numbers and that the women who attended the theater were neither simply courtesans nor aristocratic ladies; many seem to have been citizens' wives, part of that emergent group, "the middling sort," whom Gosson most explicitly addresses (Gurr 1987: 56–60). The presence of such women at the theater clearly worries Gosson, and he voices his worries in a typically paternalistic form: i.e. as a concern for woman's safety and good reputation. What Gosson argues is that the safest place for woman to be is at home, busy with household management, with neighborhood gossips, and, for recreation, with books. As he says, "The best counsel that I can give you, is to keepe home, and shun all occasion of ill speech" (Gosson 1579: F4). The dangerous place for woman to be is the theater. The interesting question is why.

Ostensibly, the threat is to woman's sexual purity. In the body of his tract Gosson argues that the theater is a place for sexual assignations; it is a "generall Market of bawdrie" (Gosson 1579: C2). Various wantons and paramours, knaves and queans "cheapen the Merchandise in that place, which they pay for elsewhere as they can agree" (Gosson 1579: C2). Presumably, any woman – and not just a prostitute – could fall prey to passion if inflamed by the allegedly lewd behaviour of the actors or by the amorous addresses of her male companions at the theater. Yet in his concluding epistle, Gosson dwells less on the possibility that the gentlewoman citizen may go away to sleep with a fellow playgoer and more on the danger posed to her by being gazed at by many men in the public space of the theater. As Gosson says: "Thought is free: you can forbidd no man, that vieweth you, to noute you and that noateth you, to judge you, for entring to places of suspition" (Gosson 1579: F2). The threat is not so much to woman's bodily purity, as to her reputation. In Gosson's account the female playgoer is symbolically whored by the gaze of many men, each woman a potential Cressida in the camp of the Greeks, vulnerable, alone, and open to whatever imputations men might cast upon her. She becomes what we might call the object of promiscuous gazing. Gosson presents the situation entirely paternalistically. For the "good" of women he warns them to stay at home, to shut themselves away from all dangers, and to find pleasure in reading or in the gossip of other women.

Yet who is endangered, really, by women's theatergoing? The intensity of Gosson's scrutiny of the woman playgoer indicates to me that her presence in the theater may have been felt to threaten more than her own purity, that in some way it put her "into circulation" in the public world of Elizabethan England in ways threatening to the larger patriarchal economy within which her circulation was in theory a highly structured process involving her passage from the house and surveillance of the father to the house and surveillance of the husband. This process was, of course, a complicated one that probably affected women of the propertied classes more severely than the daughters of laborers. It is also true that men, at least in the elite classes, often had their marriage choices determined by the father and were in no absolute sense free agents. But it was as the privileged sex that men circulated through the structures of Elizabethan society, and it was they to whom women were by and large accountable, and not vice versa. The threat the theater seems to hold for Gosson in regard to ordinary gentlewomen is that in that public space such women have become unanchored from the structures of surveillance and control "normal" to the culture and useful in securing the boundary between "good women" and "whores." Not literally passed, like Cressida, from hand to hand, lip to lip, the female spectator passes instead from eye to eye, her value as the exclusive possession of one man cheapened, put at risk, by the gazing of many eyes. To whom, in such a context, does woman belong? Are her meaning and value fixed, or fluctuating? How does one classify a woman who is not literally a whore and yet who is not, as good women were supposed to be, at home? To handle the ambiguity, the potential blurring of ideological categories, Gosson would send the gentlewoman citizen out of the theater and back to her house, husband, father, books, and gossips, where such questions admit of easier answers.

Yet I suspect the threat to the patriarchal order is even more complex than I have so far indicated. By drawing on the Cressida analogy, I have seemed to assent to Gosson's most fundamental premise, namely, that women in the theater were simply objects of scrutiny and desire, and that in that position they were in danger of being read as whores or otherwise becoming commodities outside the control of one man. But what if one reads the situation less within the horizons of masculinist ideology and asks whether women might have been empowered, and not simply victimized, by their novel position within the theater? In the theatrical economy of gazes, could men have done all the looking, held all the power? In an infamous recent American court case, Joel Steinberg was convicted of murder for beating his daughter so severely that she died of internal injuries. He had also beaten his wife, Hedda Nussbaum, in part because he could not bear the thought she was looking at him. He hit and poked her eyes with such severity that eventually artificial tearducts had to be inserted in one of them. In this case the power of the female subject "to look" caused uncontrollable rage in the man with whom she lived.[2]

The antitheatricalists frequently commented on the disruptiveness of women who came to the theater, not only because they made themselves into spectacles, but also because they became spectators, subjects who looked. Is it possible that in the theater women were licensed to look – and in a larger sense to judge what they saw and to exercise autonomy – in ways that problematized women's status as object within patriarchy? Recall, for example, Northbrooke's outraged outburst against women's presence in the theater: "what safegarde of chastitie can there be, where the woman is desired with so many eyes, where so many faces looke upon hir, and againe she uppon so manye? She must needes fire some, and hir selfe also fired againe, and she be not a Stone" (Northbrooke 1577: Jiv). Northbrooke clearly fears that women will not only inflame men, but will themselves be stirred to desire; will not only be gazed upon, but will exercise the power of looking.

In short, I am proposing that Gosson's prescriptive rhetoric may be a response, not only to a fear *for* woman, but also to a fear *of* woman, as she takes up a place in an institution which, as Steven Mullaney has argued, existed at least symbolically on the margins of authorized culture, opening space for the transformation, as much as the simple reproduction, of that culture (Mullaney 1988a: esp. 26–59). At the theater door, money changed hands in a way which enabled women access to the pleasure and privilege of gazing, certainly at the stage, and probably at the audience as well. They were therefore, as Jonson ruefully acknowledges, among those authorized to exercise their sixpence worth, or their penny's worth, of judgment. Whether or not they were accompanied by husbands or fathers, women at the theater were not "at home," but in public, where they could become objects of desire, certainly, but also desiring subjects, stimulated to want what was on display at the theater. This must have included not just sexual opportunity, but all the trappings of a commodifying culture worn upon the very backs of those attending the theater and making it increasingly difficult to discern "who one really was" in terms of the categories of a status system based on fixed and unchanging social hierarchies. As Jean-Christophe Agnew has argued, the Renaissance stage made the liquidity of social relations in a commercializing culture its theme (Agnew 1986: esp. 111–14). I would argue that the practice of playgoing may have embodied that liquidity, not simply thematized it. For Gosson good wives who took up a place at the public theater were dangerously out of their true and appropriate place, and he clearly meant to return them to that proper place by threatening those who remained in the place of danger with the name of whore. Other antitheatricalists such as Northbrooke worried obsessively, as we have seen, about "displaced persons," especially masterless men and upstart crows, people either literally uprooted, geographically, from their places of origin or symbolically uprooted through their aspirations to social places above their station. To modern eyes, women at the theater would not in any obvious sense be persons "out of place," yet for Gosson and Northbrooke they clearly were. Especially for women of the middling sort, their proper place was at home, and Gosson, like Northbrooke, used all his rhetorical skills to bully them out of the theater and back to their houses. That he was not successful suggests both the allure of theatergoing and also its potential to contribute to changing gender relations.

To understand more fully this aspect of the politics of theatergoing, it is necessary to rethink and to expand usual notions of how the public theater functioned as an ideological apparatus within English Renaissance culture. To do so requires a brief detour into contemporary theories of ideology, a detour whose implications I hope to make concrete by asking what it could have meant for women theatergoers to attend a production of a play such as Thomas Heywood's *The Wise Woman of Hogsdon*, a drama which invites thematization of the question of women as spectacle and spectator, object and agent within a culture both patriarchal and theatrical, and which invites us to speculate about the potential gap, for certain groups, between the ideological implications of a given play and the ideological consequences of playgoing.[3]

When I speak of the ideological work performed by the early modern theater, I mean simply how this institution and the plays put on there contributed to that larger ensemble of beliefs and practices comprising Elizabethan subjects' lived relations to the real. Ideology, as the obviousness of culture, is what goes without saying, what is lived as true. It is therefore precisely not a set of beliefs known to be "false" but cynically sold to others to hold them in an inferior position, nor does it originate from a conspiratorial power group (or author) bent on dominating or deceiving others. This does not mean, however, that ideology does not function to produce unequal social relations within social formations stratified by race, gender, and class, simply that ideology does not lie in anyone's conscious control, nor can it be opposed to "truth", simply to other ideological modalities of knowing. Traces of Althusserian rhetoric appear in my prose because, despite all that must be rejected and modified in the Althusserian problematic, I still find his one of the most strenuous and fruitful theorizations of ideology we have, valuable enough to warrant modification, rather than outright rejection (Althusser 1971: esp. 127–86). For Althusser the work of ideology in general is to reproduce the relations of production necessary to the survival and perpetuation of particular modes of production. It is the work of ideology to call people, interpellate them, into their positions as workers, managers, owners, rulers, and ruled, and to provide them with the subjectivities which hold them in these places with a minimum of force or coercion. Ideology thus makes people willing subjects of the dominant order.

Clearly one of the major elements of Althusser's thought needing modification is his overly deterministic view of the operations of ideology. As many have noted, elegant and therefore powerful as is Althusser's account of the operations of ideology, it does not give adequate attention to explaining change, only cultural reproduction. And it gives primacy to struggles between social classes in a way that leaves little room for the independent analysis of other modes of oppression such as those involving race and gender.[4] Anyone continuing to work with Althusser has to take account of these and other problems, partly by recognizing, with Goran Therborn, that interpellation is a process which not only subjects the subject but qualifies him or her for maneuver within the terrain of ideology (Therborn 1980: esp. 17–18), partly because no subject ever occupies only one subject position, but rather is entangled in a network of competing and contestatory ideologies. This is particularly true for complex societies in which change at different levels of the social formation occurs in a non-homologous fashion. Contradictions among the multiple positionings of the subject can therefore lead to his or her politicization, to the abandonment of particular ideological positions, and to the creation of shifting horizons of resistance.[5]

Such ideas have become increasingly important in the

ideological study of Renaissance drama in the United States as the emphasis in the early moments of new historicism on the stage as the simple agent of state power has been questioned from many quarters.[6] Now it seems more adequate to speak of the stage, not as a site simply for the dissemination of aristocratic and masculinist ideology, nor, in the mirror image of this position, as a site for a simple subversion of a social order statically and monolithically conceived as a homologous totality. Instead, scholars are trying to understand how the stage could have functioned in a more complex and contradictory fashion within the interstices of a social formation which was not static, and in which the process of ideological domination is best understood as a process of constant negotiation with, rather than simple containment of, emergent or oppositional positions. This does not mean, of course, that some interests never won out over other interests or that social conflict could be resolved in a way equally beneficial to all subjects. Rather, it implies that social struggles had various outcomes and that a simple return to the *status quo ante* was not inevitable. Sometimes subordinated groups prevailed; sometimes dominant groups prevailed only by self-transformations that made at least limited space for other interests.

This new direction in the ideological study of Renaissance theater is not, I think, simply an attempt to impose a liberationist paradigm on the stage to displace or replace a paradigm of containment. It indicates instead a recognition both of the possibilities for contradiction in the operations of the stage and the differential ways it could have impacted on various social groups. Richard Burt, for example, has stressed how the reception of productions in the public theater could not be controlled in the same way and to the same extent as productions in more explicitly courtly venues (Burt 1988: 332–46, esp. 343–5), a fact that seems acknowledged by the Act of the Common Council of London with which I began this chapter, in which the Council registered a fear that public playing removed the stabilizing contexts for reception provided by the nobleman's house or the official occasion of the wedding ceremony. Exploring similar issues, Steven Mullaney has recently suggested that the Renaissance stage, in an era when literacy was still not widespread, served to expand, for the urban populace of London, the parameters of the symbolic economy within which it moved;

he further argues that such an expansion had potentially unsettling social consequences, simply because the circulation of representations had moved beyond the control of an elite (Mullaney 1988b).

Central to much of this work is the implicit recognition that if one wishes to speak of the ideological consequences of the theater, one needs to attend to more than just theatrical representations *qua* representations, but also to the material practices and conventions of the stage and of theatergoing. As Althusser has stressed, the domain of the ideological involves more than just "ideas"; the materiality of ideology consists precisely in its embodiment in material practices (Althusser 1971: 165–70). In terms of the Renaissance theater, an emphasis upon the materiality of ideology means that it is not sufficient to talk about representations of monarchy without talking about the consequences of having those representations daily enacted by men of low estate in public amphitheaters for commercial gain (Kastan 1986: esp. 472–5); not sufficent to talk about the consequences of fables of crossdressing without considering the fact that they were enacted by men in women's clothing;[7] not sufficient to talk about the interpellation of subjects by playscripts without talking about their interpellation by the material practices of playgoing in which all people, whatever their rank or gender, were transformed into the paying customers of the emerging mercantile economy. The simplest way to put the point I wish to make is that one cannot asssume that theatrical representations have an ideological significance which is fixed and unchanging or which is unaffected by the conditions in which the representations are produced and consumed.

It has sometimes been tempting to me to think that the material practices surrounding playgoing in urban London were destabilizing to aristocratic and masculinist hegemony while the dramatic scripts themselves mostly were not. This formulation, however, is too simple. It is necessary, I think, to see that the scripts themselves embody social struggle, that they enact a contest between and a negotiation among competing ideological positions; and that a further level of analysis is also necessary as one tries to take account of the potential consonance or conflict between the ideological import of a dramatic fable and of the material conditions of its production. We cannot assume that scripts and playhouse practice ideologically reinforce one another. Sometimes they may have been in conflict, may have interpellated subjects in contradictory ways. Because Renaissance discourse about the theater focuses as much on the scene of playing as on what is performed at that scene, I believe the awkward duality with which I am wrestling is not my own invention, but a problem at some level recognized in the period itself. It seems likely that the multiple ideological levels on which the playhouse and its scripts functioned explains something about the not-quite-true feel of most attempts, both Renaissance and modern, to delineate *the* social function of the Renaissance theater. It tended, for example, as part of a commercial entertainment industry, increasingly to further in a general way the bourgeois drift of culture; yet the class politics of many of its fictions were resolutely aristocratic. This is just one of the most obvious contradictions surrounding the theater and making it difficult to say whose interests were invariably served by its practices.

Women as a group are of special interest to me, and in this chapter and the next I want to take up questions concerning their place in the theater and in theatrical representations of their theatrical practices. To begin, I turn to *The Wise Woman of Hogsdon*, a play which I want to examine briefly with a particular group of spectators in mind, Gosson's gentlewomen citizens of London. I chose this play partly because Heywood's class and gender politics are simply different from Shakespeare's and so allow one an expanded sense of the ideological possibilities of the early modern stage, partly because this play raises in particularly interesting ways the question of what *were* the ideological consequences, for women, of theatergoing. Predictably, *The Wise Woman of Hogsdon* is obsessed with issues of theatricality: its powers and its control. Class and gender conflict are, as in *Much Ado*, worked out through a struggle over the power to manipulate the world through theatrical means. In the antitheatrical tracts, of course, women were often negatively associated with theatricality and duplicity. Some of those associations are present in Heywood's text, but theatricality is also presented as a mode of empowerment for women and as a way of combating dangerous aristocratic masculinity. The play thus opens space for a less repressive and monolithic view of female theatricality than was articulated either by *Much Ado About Nothing* or by the antitheatricalists themselves.

The contradictions surrounding female power and its connection to theatrical practices center, first, on the title character. The wise woman of this text is a lower-class figure who makes her living by using her "special powers" to perform services for her neighbors, services such as finding a missing or lost object, diagnosing illness, telling the future. As Keith Thomas reports, such figures were not uncommon in English village life well into the seventeenth century. They not only performed vital physical services, such as helping women in childbirth, but they also filled a psychological gap left when the Reformation led to the abolition of certain practices, such as exorcism and confession, by which the Roman Church had allayed the common man's or woman's guilt about sin and his or her fears of demonic possession (Thomas 1971: 177–279, esp. 265). Cunning people, with their charms and medicines and prophetic powers, seemed in possession of powerful, if forbidden, knowledges, which made them anathema to the Church and to medical men, but not necessarily to ordinary people.

Often, in the polemical literature of the time, cunning people, along with witches, were presented as agents of Satan. Sometimes, as in Reginald Scot's treatise, *The Discoverie of Witchcraft*, cunning women, conjurers, exorcists, witches, and other "jugglers" were simply presented as charlatans who gained their power by tricks, illusions, and the artful leading on of their clients (Scot 1584). Heywood's wise woman is certainly a first-class swindler and charlatan. For example, when her neighbors come to her for advice, she asks leading questions to get them to tell her the details of their troubles, which she then pretends to have known in advance.

Wisewoman: And who distill'd this water?
Countryman: My wives Limbeck, if it please you.
Wisewoman: And where doth the paine hold her most?
Countryman: Marry at her heart forsooth.
Wisewoman: Ey, at her heart, shee hath a griping at her heart.
Countryman: You have hit it right.
Wisewoman: Nay, I can see so much in the Urine.
Luce 2: Just so much as is told her.
Wisewoman: Shee hath no paine in her head, hath shee?

Countryman: No indeed, I never heard her complaine of her head.

Wisewoman: I told you so, her paine lyes all at her heart; Alas good heart! but how feeles shee her stomacke?

Countryman: O queasie, and sicke at stomacke.

Wisewoman: Ey, I warrant you, I think I can see as farre into a Mill-stone as another.

(Heywood 1874: 292; II. i. 7–21)

Alternatively, she conceals herself in a closet by her front door, listening while her servant asks a client her business and then pretends to have divined that business. Essentially unlettered, she drops Latin tags and pretends to read in deep books of magical lore.

She is, then, a charlatan, and also something of a bawd. Her house is where women come to have their illegitimate babies, which the wise woman then disposes of by leaving them on the doorsteps of the wealthy. And the walls of this house contain the pictures of young women with whom a man can spend the night. Hardly the patron of the chaste, silent, and obedient, this lower-class woman traffics in flesh. This makes her house a transgressive space where deceptive and illicit activities are carried on, and which seems to put Heywood's play, ideologically, on the side of Reginald Scot and his debunking demystification of such charlatans and on the side of the many polemicists who associated women with theatricality and deceit.

Yet the class and gender politics of this play are more complicated than I have indicated. For all that the wise woman is a charlatan and her house a house of assignations, it is also the place where all members of the community come, the virtuous and the less than virtuous, and it is the place where the community's problems get solved, thanks largely to the theatrical skills of the wise woman herself. Her house becomes the site where the community's sexual and social economy is regulated, where, in essence, the predatory theatricality of Chartley, the young gallant who is the play's male protagonist, is defeated by the cleverness of a group of women. The play thus vests in their hands much of the power granted in *Much Ado* to the aristocratic Don Pedro.

Heywood's plot, despite some Byzantine overtones, is a simple one. Chartley was once contracted to marry a woman,

Luce 2, whom he abandoned practically on their marriage night. This woman, disguised as a man, tracks Chartley down and schemes to win him back by contracting herself as a servant to the wise woman and joining with the wise woman in manipulating this rogue. He, after leaving Luce 2, contracts himself to a second woman, Luce 1, virtuous daughter of a London goldsmith, whom he also abandons as he goes off in pursuit of yet a third woman, Gratiana, daughter of a wealthy knight. Chartley acts out what is presented as a dangerous instability in aristocratic male desire. He moves from woman to woman, lying to each, and ends up staging an elaborate fiction by which, on the night before his marriage to Gratiana, the knight's daughter, he goes off to sleep with Luce 1 at the wise woman's house, pretending he has been urgently called away by a dying father.

What keeps his predatory desire from ruining the lives of all these prospective brides is the cunning woman, who is presented as his antagonist from the first time they meet. These two knaves are presented as natural enemies. He calls her every sort of name – blackness, witch, hag, she-devil, sorceress, Lady Proserpine, Madam Hecate – and tries to beat her; she, in turn, vows to do anything to frustrate his desires. Twice, using highly theatrical ruses, she deceives him. The first time, when he comes to her house to marry Luce 1, she puts everyone in disguise and fools him into marrying Luce 2 and Luce 1 into marrying an earnest young suitor named Boyster, thus joining Chartley to the first object of his desire and the goldsmith's daughter to a suitably sober mate. When, still deceived into believing he has wed Luce 1, Chartley comes to sleep with her at the wise woman's house, the women stage a trick which exposes his chicanery to all those – his father, Gratiana's father, Luce 1 and Luce 2 – whom he has attempted to deceive. When he appears at her house, the wise woman puts him in a room surrounded by a circle of adjoining rooms from which he is observed by all his gulls who one by one come forward to confront him. He is left a sputtering mass of jelly, the libertine plots and deceptions of the aristocratic male exposed to everyone's gaze.

The house of the wise woman thus becomes a world upside down where women temporarily have control of men, the lower classes of the upper. Only the stigmatized lower-class figure, the cunning woman, seems to have the power to right the social world threatened by gentlemanly profligacy and theatricality.

Fire drives out fire. Yet the role of the two Luces deserves further attention. Significantly, Luce 1, while somewhat inexplicably the wise woman's friend, is kept in ignorance by her throughout the play. Luce 1 has all the respectability the wise woman lacks and none of her power. She is chaste, fairly silent, and obedient. An early scene finds her lamenting to an apprentice the fact she must sit in public to mind her father's shop, a position which exposes her to the gaze of many men, a position she abhors.

> I doe not love to sit thus publikely:
> And yet upon the traffique of our Wares,
> Our provident Eyes and presence must still wayte.
> Doe you attend the shop, Ile ply my worke.
> I see my father is not jelous of me,
> That trusts mee to the open view of all.
> The reason is, hee knowes my thoughts are chast,
> And my care such, as that it needes the awe
> Of no strict Overseer.
>
> (I. ii. 4–12)

This good daughter of the patriarchy speaks at once to every suitor of marriage; and her marriage choice, Chartley, is directly referred by her to her father to ask his permission. Unlike the stereotypical merchants found in many city comedies, Luce and her father are not rich. They are, simply, virtuous citizens devoid of guile. Importantly, they are also powerless in the face both of Chartley's manipulations and the wise woman's. Significantly, Luce 1 does not even know that because of the disguises worn at her wedding she has not married Chartley, but Boyster, the mate she finds herself wedded to at play's end.

That compliance with dominant codes of feminine virtue results in powerlessness and domination is strikingly revealed by the presence in the play of Luce 1's double, the aggressively different Luce 2. Of this woman we know little but that she is a "gentlewoman," left her father's house when abandoned by Chartley, and is absolutely tenacious in her pursuit of this feckless gallant. For most of the play, she dresses as a male page – a theatrical disguise she uses to achieve power over Chartley. In fact, she wears women's clothing only when participating in the plot to trick him into marrying her instead of Luce 1. The power she symbolically assumes by adopting male dress is further indicated by the fact that she is the instigator of much of the plotting that goes on at the wise woman's. She and the cunning woman are the primary architects of the two great scenes of theatrical cozenage: the double wedding where the Jacks get only the Jills Luce 2 and the wise woman have assigned to them, and the climactic scene in which before one audience after another Chartley has his lying ways exposed. As is so often true in this period, power is shown to lie with the theatrically skillful, and in this play the most theatrically skillful figures are women. If the wise woman outsmarts and out-deceives Chartley, lower-class feminine theatricality outstripping his entrepreneurial shapeshifting, the wise woman is in turn outsmarted by the chaste, if hardly silent and compliant, Luce 2, who does not reveal her female sex to the wise woman until the last deception has been played out and Luce 2 claims Chart-ley for her own, her desire gratified as Luce 1's was not. In the hierarchy of power and knowledge which emerges in the play, Luce 2 is at the very top, and she is the transgressive figure of the woman in man's attire seemingly free from the control of a father or husband.

Of course, it is easy to see a reining in of the subversive impulses of the play in its denouement. This is particularly true concerning Luce 2 who, having spent much of the play in breeches and free of overt patriarchal control, at play's end willingly enters what will in all likelihood be a patriarchal mar-riage and doffs her breeches and with them, perhaps, her power. Moreover, her being a gentlewoman affirms class privilege even as she subverts gender hierarchy. It is, after all, the gentlewoman whose desire is gratified, and not the desire of the goldsmith's daughter. Moreover, the play ends up affirming patriarchal mar-riage three times over, and, rather than class antagonism, con-cludes with a utopian image of class reconciliation as Chartley blesses his enemy the wise woman, and the union of Luce 1 and Boyster marks the non-predatory alliance of citizen and gentleman classes.

Despite these obviously recuperative elements, the play reveals the constructed and interested nature of the social order by showing subordinated groups successfully occupying the positions and clothing and wielding the powers of the domi-nators, including their use of theatrical practices to control the world. While it is difficult to construe the play as advocating the dismantling of either the patriarchal system or the class sytem, in several ways it invites disidentification with both. This is not only because it shows men, and gentlemen, as no more inherently and naturally capable of wielding power than women and lower-class figures, thus undermining the "natural" justification for their privileges, but the play also is traversed by competing understandings of the same phenomena which show the implicit contest between ideological positions. For example, while the wise woman is inscribed within a discourse of the charlatan – even by Luce 2 – she is also clearly inscribed within a discourse of Rabelaisian carnal materiality and associated with the homeostatic regulation of the social and sexual economy of the play. Likewise, while Luce 1 is inscribed within the discourse of the good woman familiar from the conduct books, Luce 2 is her transgressive double, embodying an alternative to, and demystification of, her sister. This play's climactic scene presents the highly entertaining spectacle of a man observed, manipulated, and humiliated by the women he has tried to wrong. And this male is ultimately made subject to the desire of the woman who has most aggressively and transgressively sought him. Moreover, that woman has attained her desire, chastely, within the house of a bawd, co-operating with, but distancing herself from, the wise woman, maneuvering between the powerlessness of Luce 1 and the victimization of those nameless women whose babies the cunning woman left on the doorsteps of the rich. The play is thus a site for ideological contestation and negotiation and not merely for the reproduction of dominant ideologies. While it concludes with an image of harmony and utopian resolution of class and gender struggle, it has recorded traces of that struggle.

And what of the female spectator to this fiction? Her experience must have been complicated. Though invited by cultural discourses such as Gosson's to take herself off, like a good Luce 1, to her father's house, to flee the promiscuous gazing of men, and to wait for a husband to be delivered to her, the female playgoer nonetheless *was* in the theater, in this instance watching a fiction that walks a fine line between returning women to their "proper places" and validating them as desiring, active subjects. If Heywood's text in part enacts, in order to allay, masculine anxiety about women who exercise control over themselves and over men, it is not clear that female spectators would focus only on the recuperative dimensions of that fiction.

If male spectators focused on the play's palliating ending, is it not possible that at least some women might have focused on what went before: namely, the wise woman's successful domination of her aristocratic enemy and Luce 2's successful achievement of her desire? It is of course true that Luce 2's desire is channeled into marriage, *the* patriarchal institution giving woman her cultural definition. That acknowledged, it seems also necessary to acknowledge how far Luce 2 breaks away from the model of "proper" femininity offered by Luce 1.

Moreover, as a playgoer, the female spectator was, as Northbrooke and Gosson feared, being interpellated into a subject position potentially at odds with the patriarchal injunctions governing the behavior of a "good" woman such as Luce 1. The female spectator to *The Wise Woman of Hogsdon* was, in Gosson's terms, within "the market of bawdrie," the public playhouse, a site, I would argue, as ideologically complicated – for women – as the wise woman's own complex establishment. In this place of licensed gazing, men and women alike were spectacles and spectators, desired and desiring. Even when this theater, through its fictions, invited women to take up the subordinate positions masculine ideology defined as proper for them, the very practice of playgoing put women in positions potentially unsettling to patriarchal control. To be part of urban public life as spectator, consumer, and judge moved the gentlewoman citizen outside of that domestic enclosure to which Gosson would return her. While it does no good to exaggerate the powers of women in such a situation, I think the antitheatrical polemicists were right to worry about female theatergoing, though not only for the reasons they were able to articulate. Focusing on the danger *to* women, Gosson elides the threat posed to patriarchal power *by* women who occupied novel positions in the urban culture of Renaissance London.

It has long been debated whether women as a group lost or gained power during the Renaissance. It is a truism of Marxist historiography that capitalism pushed women out of certain spheres of economic production and into disempowered positions within the reconstituted nuclear family that was to become dominant during the ascendency of the bourgeoisie.[8] Yet the enclosure of women within the private sphere did not happen all at once; nor did it happen evenly across various class and status groups. As Catherine Belsey has argued, the early seventeenth century was a period of general social struggle and transformation, including heightened tension over the place of women and the proper functioning of the gender system (Belsey 1985a). It would be naive to assume that at this time patriarchy simply broke down; it seems equally naive to assume that its control over all women, in all places, was equally absolute. I have been suggesting in this chapter that especially for urban women of the "middling sort," changing cultural practices, including but not limited to, the emergence of the public theater, opened space for female behavior which men found genuinely threatening to their construction of proper womanhood. I think Gosson's unspoken fear was that the practice of female theater-going, the entry of the middle-class woman into the house of Proteus, could spur her transformation from the compliant and powerless fantasy object, Luce 1, into the transgressive, desiring subject, Luce 2. In the very display of patriarchal anxiety one can see traces of gender struggle whose outcome could not have been known in advance, any more than can the outcome of social struggles in our own time. Only with the benefit of hindsight can one see how firmly patriarchal bourgeois culture eventually reasserted control over women, instantiating them within the home and within the scopic economy of the male gaze. But it might have been otherwise, as the nervous rhetoric of a Gosson suggests.

5

POWER AND EROS
Crossdressing in dramatic representation and theatrical practice

The complexity of social struggles in the period, particularly those surrounding gender, and the complexity of the public theater's participation in those struggles, can be teased out still further by looking next at the theater's involvement in one of the most overtly stigmatized practices enumerated in the antitheatrical tracts; namely, crossdressing.[1] Again, this phenomenon can not be approached solely on the level of representation. There are many female characters who dress as men in Renaissance drama, and a smaller number of men who assume the clothes of women. On the other hand, every single performance of a public-theater play involved members of an all-male acting troupe putting on female attire in order to "personate" whatever women characters a given play might specify. As we have seen, it was this confounding of sexual "kinds" on the actor's part that particularly roused the fury of a Northbrooke, a Stubbes, a Prynne.

In looking at representations of crossdressing in stage plays along with the practice of boy actors dressing as women, I will, as in chapter 4, explore possible ideological gaps and discontinuities, as well as homologies, between the various levels of theatrical practice. The stage, I want to keep insisting, did not do its ideological work in a seamless manner. In this chapter I am also going to place theatrical crossdressing in relation to actual instances of crossdressing in the London streets and in relation to the polemical controversy surrounding the "unnatural," mannishly attired woman. Of course, evoking the social world of contemporary London will not "explain" theatrical crossdressing in the sense of providing it with either an origin or a fixed meaning. As part of a stage action, the ideological import of crossdressing was mediated by all the conventions of dramatic narrative and dramatic production. It cannot simply be conflated with crossdressing on the London streets or with instances of crossdressing in disciplining rituals such as chari-vari and skimington. As with any social practice, the meaning of crossdressing varied with the circumstances of its occurrence, with the particulars of the institutional or cultural sites of its enactment, and with the class position of the transgressor. None-theless, while paying attention in what follows to the *differences* among various manifestations of crossdressing in Renaissance culture, I want to suggest that taken together they tell us some-thing about both class and gender struggles in the period and about the complex role of the theater in those struggles.[2]

At the simplest level, the polemical, monarchical, and theatri-cal preoccupation with crossdressing in the period from roughly 1580 to 1620 signaled a gender system under pressure. As fact and as idea, crossdressing threatened a normative social order based upon strict principles of hierarchy and subordination, of which woman's subordination to man was a chief instance, trumpeted from pulpit, instantiated in law, and acted upon by monarch and commoner alike. Yet, of course, the subversive or transgressive potential of this practice could be and was recuperated in a number of ways. Many plays participated in that recuperative process. This chapter, however, will not simply be a tale of containment triumphant, in part because the most radical implications of female crossdressing *do* find embodiment in certain plays of the period. And other, less radical, crossdress-ing dramas nonetheless implicitly enlarge the prerogatives of some women within an overarching patriarchal framework. In addition, the theatrical fact of the all-male acting troupe con-tained an ever-present challenge to the essentialized categories of male and female that were in some cases put at risk by representations of crossdressing and, in other cases, were con-firmed by them. In short, a gap could open between the ideology embodied in representation and that in theatrical practice. Just as importantly, the fact of boy actors presented an ever-present challenge to the channeling of erotic energy into exclusively heterosexual forms, a channeling *also* put at risk in some crossdressing fictions but, more often, enacted through them. To unpack these matters will be the work of the latter part of this chapter, but first to some historical questions.

*

First, how many people crossdressed in early modern England? There is probably no way empirically to answer such a question. Given Biblical prohibitions against the practice and their frequent repetition from the pulpit and in the prescriptive literature of the period, one would guess that the number of people who dared walk the streets of London in the clothes of the other sex was limited. Nonetheless, there *are* records of women, in particular, who did so, and who were punished for offenses, such as prostitution, associated with crossdressing. From at least 1580 to 1620 preachers and polemicists kept up a steady attack on the practice. In 1620 James I ordered the preachers of London to inveigh from the pulpit against the practice of women dressing mannishly in the London streets. That year also saw the publication of the two polemical tracts, *Hic Mulier* and *Haec Vir*, which attacked and defended crossdressing, and which suggest it had become a practice taken up with particular enthusiasm by the fashion-mongering wives of the City who are accused in the tracts of simultaneously transgressing class and gender boundaries. By wearing ever more ornate clothing, they encroached on the privileges of aristocratic women; and by wearing men's clothing they encroached on the privileges of the advantaged sex. As we have seen, even in the late 1570s, antitheatricalists had attacked crossdressing by boy actors, and often these attacks had spilled over into the denigration of women who dressed mannishly or above their station. In his *The Description of England* William Harrison railed against the accelerating decline of modesty and decorum in dress, ending his diatribe against improperly dressed women by remarking that "I have met with some of these trulls in London so disguised that it passed my skill to discern whether they were men or women" (Harrison 1587; rpt 1968: 147). The word "trull" is important. The OED defines "trulle" as "a low prostitute, or concubine; a drab, strumpet, trollop." Harrison's diction links the mannish woman with prostitution, and there were strong discursive linkages throughout the period between female crossdressing and the threat of female sexual incontinence.

By examining records from Bridewell and the Aldermen's Court between about 1565 and 1605, R. Mark Benbow has indeed found that many of the women apprehended in men's clothing during the period were accused of prostitution.[3] For example, on 3 July 1575 the Aldermen's Court records report that one Dorothy Clayton, spinster, "contrary to all honesty and womanhood commonly goes about the City apparelled in man's atire. She has abused her body with sundry persons and lived an incontinent life. On Friday she is to stand on the pillory for two hours in men's apparell and then to be sent to Bridewell until further order" (Rep. 19, 93). Of Margaret Wakeley in 1601 the Bridewell records read: "[she] had a bastard child and went in man's apparell" (Minute Book 4, 207). Of other women it was simply said that they were apprehended dressed as men, though clearly the suspicion was that any woman so apprehended probably led a loose life. One woman, Johanna Goodman, along with her husband, was whipped and sent to Bridewell in 1569 simply for dressing as a male servant so she could accompany her soldier husband to war (Aldermen's Court, Rep. 16, 522).[4] It is impossible to tell the "class" position of many of these women. Most appear to be unmarried women of the serving class eking out a precarious living in London. Some are recorded as being "in service" to various London tavernkeepers and tradesmen. Some may have worn male clothing for protection in traveling about in the city; some may have been driven to prostitution by economic necessity, with their crossdressed apparel becoming a demonized "sign" of their enforced sexual availability. It is tempting to speculate that if citizen wives of the Jacobean period assumed men's clothes as a sign of their wealth and independence, lower-class women may well have assumed them from a sense of vulnerability, with an eventual turn to prostitution merely marking the extent of that vulnerability.

That actual women of several social classes *did* crossdress in Renaissance England is an important fact, but equally important is how their behavior was ideologically processed or rendered intelligible in the discourses of the time. Specifically, what made adopting the dress of the other sex so transgressive that it was regularly read as a sign of the criminality of lower-class women and a cause for middle-class women to be harangued by preachers or husbands? Most simply, crossdressing, like other disruptions of the Renaissance semiotics of dress, opened a gap between the supposed reality of one's social station and sexual kind, and the clothes that were to display that reality to the world. Through its sumptuary proclamations the state attempted to regulate dress in early modern England, especially in urban settings, precisely to keep people in the social "places" to which they were born (Hooper 1915: 433–49). These edicts state who could wear certain colors (such as purple), certain fabrics (such as silk), and certain adornments (such as spurs, daggers, jewels). In myriad ways, clothes distinguished one social group from those both above and below; they were precise indicators of status and degree. To transgress the codes governing dress disrupted an official view of the social order in which one's identity was largely determined by one's station or degree – and where that station was, in theory, providentially determined and immutable.

As Stephen Orgel has pointed out (1992: 14), sumptuary laws regulated class mobility; they did not specifically criminalize gender crossdressing. Yet as we have seen, in the antitheatrical tracts sartorial infractions of status and gender boundaries were seen as linked moral transgressions; and in court cases female crossdressing seems to be read as a generalized marker of criminality. Among the antitheatricalists, Stubbes, for example, worried about the way inappropriate dress could erase divinely ordered social distinctions. You will recall his plaintive exclamation that "there is such a confuse mingle mangle of apparell in Ailgna, and such preposterous excesse therof, as every one is permitted to flaunt it out, in what apparell he lust himselfe, or can get by anie kind of meanes. So that it is verie hard to knowe, who is noble, who is worshipfull, who is a gentleman, who is not" (Stubbes 1583: C2ᵛ). In short, when rules of apparel are violated, class distinctions break down. But so do gender distinctions. The antitheatricalists urged women and boy actors not to wear the clothes of the opposite sex because to do so confounded the visible distinctions separating one sexual kind from another. As Stubbes elsewhere says: "Our Apparell was given us as a signe distinctive to discern betwixt sex and sex, and therefore one to weare the Apparel of another sex, is to participate with the same, and to adulterate the verities of his owne kinde" (Stubbes 1583: F5ᵛ). In *Hic Mulier* the crossdressed woman is enjoined to "Remember how your Maker made for our first Parents coates, not one coat, but a coat for the man, and a coat for the woman; coates of severall fashions, severall formes, and for several uses; the mans coat fit for his labour, the womans fit for her modestie" (B2ᵛ-B3). To switch coats is to undo the work of heaven.

Stephen Greenblatt, drawing on the work of Thomas Laqueur, has recently argued that modern notions of sexual difference really originate later than the Renaissance and that in at least some Renaissance discourses there appears to be only one sex, women being but imperfectly formed or incomplete men. Greenblatt then goes on to argue that a transvestite theater was a natural, indeed, almost an inevitable, product of such a culture (Greenblatt 1988: 88). Stubbes and the other antitheatrical writers suggest that a transvestite theater could also be read, in the Renaissance, as *un*natural, as a transgression of a divinely sanctioned social order. What are we to make of this seeming contradiction? First, it suggests the need to recognize the plurality of discourses about gender in the Renaissance.[5] If dominant medical discourses saw only male genitalia in both men and women and so, in some sense, authorized the view that there was only one sex, the Bible provided authority, seized by Stubbes, for a two-sex gender system: "Male and female created he them" (Genesis 1: 27). In some discourses, masculine and feminine identity *were* seen as points on a continuum, not separate essences, but in works such as the antitheatrical tracts the language of two kinds predominates, and the injunction from Deuteronomy against wearing the clothes of the other sex is repeated with tiresome frequency.

I think the real point is that the Renaissance needed the idea of two genders, one subordinate to the other, as a key part of its hierarchical view of the social order and to buttress its gendered division of labor. The interesting possibility raised by Laqueur's work is that gender differences may not in the Renaissance have always or necessarily been built upon a self-evident notion of biological sexual difference as was to be true in the nineteenth century (Laqueur 1990: 25–148). That simply means that gender difference and hierarchy had to be produced and secured – through ideological interpellation when possible, through force when necessary – on other grounds. If women were not inevitably depicted as anatomically different from men in some essential way, they could be seen as different merely by virtue of their lack of masculine perfection (softer, weaker, less hot) and their subordination justified on those grounds. Then, as now, gender relations, however eroticized, were relations of power, produced and held in place through enormous cultural labor in the interests of the dominant gender. In the early modern period the regulation of dress was part of this apparatus for producing and marking gender difference, though increasingly, as I will suggest, with the production of bourgeois interiority, the marks of gender difference were not to be inscribed solely on the outside of the body through apparel but to be worn inwardly and made manifest through a properly gendered subjectivity.

Catherine MacKinnon has argued that the modern emphasis on sexual difference – as used to justify separate and unequal spheres of work and experience – has obscured the political realities of domination and exploitation that have continued to regulate the relations between the genders (MacKinnon 1987: 32–45). By contrast, the Renaissance was forthright about man's proper domination of women. Discourses of gender in the Renaissance were overwhelmingly hierarchical. Men and women were first and foremost described as dominant and subservient, perfect and less perfect, fit for rule and unfit for rule. But this unceasing emphasis on man's proper lordship over woman found ready justification in appeals to differences between men and women in regard to their capacity to reason, to control passion, etc. In short, languages of difference – though not necessarily biological anatomical difference – were useful in underpinning gender hierarchy, and keeping that hierarchy in place was not done without struggle. As with conflicts over social mobility, gender struggles were in part played out on the terrain of dress.

Disruptions of the semiotics of dress by those placed high and those placed low on the gender hierarchy were not, however, read in the same way. For a man, wearing women's dress undermined the authority supposedly belonging to the superior sex. It might indicate that a man had been in some way "o'ermastered" by a woman, either beaten in battle by her, as Artegall was, or overwhelmed by uncontrollable amorous desire for her, as was Antony. In such cases, wearing women's clothes shamed the man by indicating a fall from his "natural" position of dominance and control. Phillip Stubbes, of course, was less concerned with shaming rituals, of which he would probably have approved, than with men's *voluntary* assumption of female dress or simply of overly ornate clothing. Nostalgic as ever for a romanticized past, Stubbes proclaimed that the wearing of effeminately ornate clothing shows that men of the modern age are "weake, tender and infirme, not able to abide such sharp conflicts and blustering stormes" (Stubbes 1583: E) as their forefathers had endured or those men of the modern age who abstained from "excessive wering of silks, velvets, satens, damasks, taffeties and such like" (Stubbes 1583: E^v).[6] Wearing women's clothing, as opposed to merely ornate clothing, represented a further step in debasement. Transvestite actors appalled Stubbes because they contaminated the boundary separating male and female "kinds," mixing high with low. This is such a debasement of man's proper place that Stubbes and other antitheatricalists could only make such men into monsters, sometimes by implying they were sodomites.

In the antitheatrical tracts, as in anti-Catholic polemic in which priestly vestments were read as a kind of female clothing, men wearing women's clothing are accused of engaging in unnatural sexual practices, for which the catch-all designation was sodomy.[7] Of course, as Alan Bray points out, while sodomy in theory was a heinous offense, there were relatively few sodomy prosecutions during the period (Bray 1988: 71). Moreover the crime seems in daily life seldom to have been associated with what we would now term ordinary homosexual activity, for which there is quite a bit of evidence in the period, especially between men of unequal status or in clear positions, respectively, of dependency and control, such as master and servant, schoolmen and students. Nonetheless, sodomy remained a strong cultural designation for the unnatural, and men accused of wearing women's clothing were discursively placed at the outer margins of society by recourse to this language of sexual monstrosity and criminality.

For women, the significance of crossdressing was different. In the polemical literature women who crossdressed were less often accused of engaging in unnatural sexual practices than of being sexually incontinent, that is, of being whores. This was in part because the discursive construction of woman in the Renaissance involved seeing her as a creature of strong sexual appetites needing strict regulation. Her sexual desire was both mark of her inferiority and justification for her control by men. As Peter Stallybrass has argued, discipline and control of woman's body were central patriarchal preoccupations (Stallybrass 1986: 123–42). The orifices of that body were to be policed, its actions circumscribed. Women who gadded about outside the home or who talked too much (by male standards), were suspected of being whores – the open door and the open mouth signifying sexual incontinence, as well. The good woman was closed off: silent, chaste, and immured within the home. As Edmund Tilney primly enjoined married women seeking to preserve good reputations: "The chiefest way for a woman to preserve and maintaine this good fame, is to bee resident in her own house" (Tilney 1587: E2^v). When women took men's clothes, they symbolically left their subordinate positions and enclosed spaces. They became mobile, masterless women, and this threatened overthrow of hierarchy was discursively read as the eruption of uncontrolled sexuality.

The *Hic Mulier* tract of 1620 presents most clearly this particular construction of the crossdressed woman and the kinds of repression it elicited. Predictably, crossdressed women are accused in the tract of excessive sexual appetite. With their wanton feathers, broad-brimmed hats, and French doublets "all unbutton'd to entice," they "give a most easie way to every luxurious action" (A4^v). Along with giving over their long hair and their sewing needles, they have given over modesty, silence, and chastity. Moreover, such women signal not only the breakdown of the hierarchical gender system, but of the class system as well. The author calls them "but ragges of Gentry," "the adulterate branches of rich Stocks," "all base, all barbarous" (B). The mannish woman not only produces bastards but is one, and threatens the collapse of the entire class system. The very state itself is represented as threatened by her behavior. The author writes: "If this [crossdressing] bee not barbarous, make the rude Scithian, the untamed Moore, the naked Indian, or the wilde Irish, Lords and Rulers of well governed Cities" (B^v). In a stunning revelation of racial and national chauvinism, the aspiration of women beyond their places is associated with the monstrous notion of the black in rulership over the white, the Irish over the English. Such consequences – though imagined only – invite reprisal. Predictably, what is evoked at the end is the power of the state and of the patriarch within the family to quell woman's unruliness. The author wants the "powerfull Statute of apparell but lift up his Battle-Axe, and crush the offenders in pieces, so as every one may bee knowne by the true badge of their bloud, or Fortune" (C^v). For when women "catch the bridle in their teeth, and runne away with their Rulers, they care not into what dangers they plunge either their Fortunes or Reputations" (C2); consequently, those who are "Fathers, Husbands, or Sustainers of these new Hermaphrodites" (C2ᵛ) must keep them in order, forbid the buying of such outrageous apparel, and instruct them in the virtues which are women's best ornaments. It is important to remember that for the poor woman who found herself in the Aldermen's Court, it was not just a husband's chastisement, but the whip, pillory, and prisons of the state's repressive apparatuses that constituted her as a guilty subject and effected her punishment for the criminality for which her crossdressed condition was taken as a sign or mark.

What I am going to suggest is that these worries about the unruly crossdressed woman, and the various means of control devised to contain the threat she constituted, signal, as Karen Newman, Catherine Belsey, and others have suggested, that early modern England was not only experiencing major trans-formations of its economic infrastructure, with attendant dislo-cations of social relations among different class and status groups, but experiencing disturbing dislocations of the gender system, as well (Belsey 1985a: 129–221; Newman 1991: 40–41). Social historians have found that in some areas, particularly where economic change was most rapid and changes in family form were most pronounced, the disciplining and restraint of women increased during this period, sometimes taking the form of an increased regulation of women's sexuality. Martin Ingram has argued, for example, that the period 1580–1620 witnessed an increase in the prosecution of prenuptial pregnancies, and an increasing preoccupation with the strains placed on the com-monweal by bastards (1985a: 147–9). By 1620 it was common, as it had not been before, for a woman who produced a bastard to be jailed for up to a year (Ingram 1985a: 155).

But not all the disciplining of women went on through the ecclesiastical or civil courts. Charivaris, skimingtons, or rough ridings were communal rituals through which unruly women were disciplined and insufficiently dominating husbands reproved.[8] The charivari specifically punished a woman's viola-tion of her place in the gender hierarchy. Sometimes she had merely "worn the breeches" in the sense of ordering her hus-band about; sometimes she was accused of beating her spouse; sometimes of having made him a cuckold. The punishment was, in the first instance, symbolic. The couple's inversion of gender hierarchy was mirrored by having the husband ride backward on a horse through the town while neighbours played cacophonous music. Husband beating was specifically punished by having what was often a substitute for the husband hold a distaff while riding backward on a horse. Meanwhile a woman figure, a Lady Skimington (often a man dressed as a woman), beat him with a ladle used for making butter and cheese. Transvestitism, symbolic inversions such as riding backwards, and rough music were all ways of registering that important cultural boundaries had been erased, important social hierarchies disrupted, by the offending parties. Similarly, women who talked too much, who were "scolds," were put upon a cucking stool and dunked in water to stop the incontinence of the mouth (Boose 1991).

David Underdown has argued that in the century between 1560 and 1660 there are many signs of an increased use of charivaris and the cucking stool, especially in communities where traditional modes of ordering society along vertical lines of hierarchy, deference, and paternalism were being disrupted and displaced by what we associate more with the modern horizontal alignment of people within classes and with the rise of protocapitalist economic practices (Underdown 1985: 116–36). The upland wood and pasture areas of the west counties, for example, where there was a strong influx of migrant labor, where extended families were dispersed into separate, highly nucleated households, and where capitalism had penetrated in terms of the heavy reliance on the putting-out system of cloth manufacture, evidenced more occurrences of charivaris, etc., than did the more centralized village communities of the grain-growing valleys where the population was more stable, families less nucleated, and the pace of social change less rapid. Cities were another site of gender tension, in part simply because they uprooted people from traditional social structures. As many have noted, in times of general social dislocation, fears about change are often displaced onto women (Jardine 1983: 162). Cities also created new and unsettling positions for middle-class women, in particular, to occupy. As was discussed in chapter 4, city women could engage in urban pleasures such as going to the theater or buying the commodities produced by English trade and manufacture (Thirsk 1978). Some came to occupy positions of economic power as widows of merchants or as visible workers in their husband's shops. A foreign visitor to London, Thomas Platter, noted in 1599 how much freedom English women had vis-à-vis their continental counterparts (Harbage 1941: 76–7). But this freedom, I have been arguing, was unsettling to the patriarchal order. The calls at the end of *Hic Mulier* for the reining in of women's freedom are but one sign of just how unsettling change in the gender system had become.

Ironically, if the vast social changes of the period led to intensified pressures on women and in many cases to a strengthening of patriarchal authority in the family and the state, these changes also produced sites of resistance and possibilities of new powers for some women.[9] While new strategies were constantly devised to control women and reaffirm their subordination, they did not all succeed, or succeeded only at the cost of concessions in some areas. For example, while the emergence of a print culture and the slow increase in women's literacy during the early modern period provided new means for interpellating women as good subjects of the patriarchal order, as witnessed by the outpouring of books on housewifery and female piety after the 1580s (Hull 1982), nonetheless increased literacy allowed some women access to authorities (such as Scripture), and to technologies (such as print) that enabled them to begin to rewrite their inscriptions within patriarchy.[10] To take another example, consider the contradictions of Protestant marriage theory. As William and Malleville Haller suggested in the 1940s, Protestant marriage ideology provided a vehicle for giving new cultural importance to marriage and to the home as the chief seat of patriarchal authority. But in investing the home and marriage with new importance, Protestant theologians ended up elevating woman's position as keeper of that home and as the spiritual equal of her husband (Haller 1941–2: 235–72). This elevation undermined starkly hierarchical theories of gender and opened space for ideas of negotiation, mutuality, and contract between husband and wife, some of which mutuality we may sense being worked out in Shakespeare's romantic comedies.[11]

All of this, I think, has bearing on how we are to evaluate the various forms of crossdressing detailed at the beginning of this chapter. In a period of social dislocation in which the gender system was one of the major sites of anxiety and change, female crossdressing in any context had the *potential* to raise fears of women wearing the breeches and undermining the hierarchical social order, though obviously women of different social classes had quite different opportunities and resources for making changes in that system. In the *Haec Vir* tract the mannish woman declares that not nature, but custom, dictates women's dress and women's subservient place in society and that, moreover, "Custome is an idiot" (1620: B2^v). No matter that the tract changes direction and ends up with the familiar plea that if men would be more mannish, women would return to their accustomed role; the fact remains that through the discussion of women's dress emerged a strong and subversive reading of the conventionality of the whole gender system.

The subversive potential of women dressed as men was self-consciously exploited in other cultural contexts as well. Natalie Davis has documented that crossdressed figures were prominent both in carnival – where gender and class boundaries were tested and confirmed – and in food riots, demonstrations against enclosures, and other forms of lower-class protest (Davis 1978: 154–5, 176–83). In such activities men sometimes performed as Lady Skimingtons, appropriating the powerful iconography of the unruly woman for their own purposes, as in the anti-enclosure riots that formed what has become known as the Western Rising of 1626–32 (Sharp 1980: 4). Clearly crossdressing had enormous symbolic significance, and the state had an interest in controlling it. Witness James's injunction to the preachers of London that they condemn the practice. The issue I will address in the rest of this chapter concerns the role of theatrical representations and enactments of crossdressing in the gender struggles of the period. Did the theater, for example, with its many fables of crossdressing, form part of the cultural apparatus for policing gender boundaries or did it serve as a site for their further disturbance? If women off the stage seized the language of dress to act out transgressions of the gender system, did the theater effectively co-opt this transgression by transforming it into fictions which depoliticized the practice? Or was the theater in some sense an agent of cultural transform-ation, helping to create new subject positions and gender relations for men and women in a period of rapid social change? And how did the all-male mode of dramatic production – the fact of crossdressing as a daily part of dramatic practice – affect the ideological import of these fictions of crossdressing? To answer these questions I want to move away from the broad and unnuanced picture of gender dislocation I have been painting to the specifics of particular texts and of women's interpellation as gendered and eroticized subjects at the site of the stage.

I start with the obvious: most Renaissance plays depicting crossdressing, with the exception of a few works such as *The Roaring Girl*, do not in any direct way constitute "comments" on the crossdressing debates. The plays are not topical in that way, and in employing crossdressing motifs they are using a staple of comic tradition with a long dramatic lineage. Nonetheless, many crossdressing plays are intensely preoccupied with threats to the gender system. Collectively, they play a role in producing and managing anxieties about women on top, women who are not "in their places," but are gadding, gossiping, and engaging – it is assumed – in extramarital sex, and in managing anxieties about the fragility of male authority. Moreover, while the thrust of many of these plays is toward containing threats to the traditional gender system, this is not uniformly so. As sites of social struggle conducted through discourse, these plays vary markedly in their ideological implications.

At one extreme, consider *Epicoene*. This is a play saturated with the fear of women who have moved or might move from their proper place of subordination, and it points to some of the changing social conditions that made such movement a possibility and a threat. Specifically the play, set in contemporary London and produced in 1608 for the boy's company at Whitefriars, shows how the emerging metropolis offers new opportunities for women to be other than chaste, silent, and obedient. Prominent are the Collegians, a coterie of "masculine" women who live away from their husbands, gad about London, and spend money on the consumer goods (such as coaches) and commercial pastimes (such as theater) increasingly available in the City. Money, mobility, and the presence of other women in similar circumstances allow the Collegians to form a society in which female tastes prevail and the authority of men, specifically husbands, is flouted. Masculine authority is further undermined by Mistress Otter, a woman who brought a sizeable fortune to her marriage with the sea captain, Tom Otter, and through a favorable marriage contract has retained control of much of that money and consequently of her spouse. As she reminds him, he agreed that she "would be a princess and reign in mine own house, and you would be my subject and obey me" (Jonson 1966: 52, III. i. 29–30). The unnaturalness of her relation to the henpecked Tom Otter is a major part of the play's misogynist humor. Though not literally crossdressed, all of these women symbolically presume to masculine rule and, predictably, display the devouring appetites (for food, drink, things, sex) associated with women who have taken the bit in their teeth and run from their masters.

The play's misogyny finds its most complex expression through the figure of Morose. Morose hates everything about the bustling world of London which, ironically, he depends upon for his wealth. He especially hates the thought of marrying a bossy, noisy London wife, but he needs a wife to insure that he can control the passage of his wealth to his own heir and not to his nephew, Dauphine. He wants to exploit woman's reproductive labor but senses that marriage – at least in London – may implicate him in a complicated and precarious relationship. Cleverly, Dauphine uses male crossdressing – a man impersonating a woman to be Morose's wife – to fulfill Morose's fantasy of finding a silent and compliant wife. Epicoene hardly speaks at all, and when s/he does, it is in a whisper. Importantly, she promises to spend Morose's wealth, not to fulfill her own desires, as the Collegians do, but to display *his* tastes and *his* position. Even her tailors, as is true of the tailor in Petruchio's country house in *The Taming of the Shrew*, will take their directions from the master, in this case from Morose (II. v. 66–82). The control of female dress is thus again singled out as a crucial terrain on which masculine authority will be affirmed.

Importantly, Dauphine uses the crossdressed figure of Epicoene to fill the position and place of an actual wife with a masculine construction of female perfection, and, after the marriage, uses the same figure to embody a demonized version of female misrule as Epicoene joins the Collegians and outdoes them in filling Morose's house with noise, food, and luxuries. It is crucial to recognize that in resolving his power struggle with his uncle over money, Dauphine does not cure his uncle of misanthropy and misogyny, but exploits these traits and exacerbates them. He outwits his uncle, not with the help of women, but at their expense, as the man playing Epicoene

usurps woman's person and place to act out degrading masculine constructions of her. In the end, the whole problem of the
complexities of right rule in marriage – in the urban setting of
London – is sidestepped. "The wife" turns into a man; neither
Dauphine nor Morose marries; and property conveniently
passes to the next generation without the disruptive agency of
woman having anywhere to be openly acknowledged. In this
instance, male crossdressing becomes a way to appropriate, and
then erase, the troubling figure of the wife.

It may be important, moreover, that this play of troubled and
parodied marriages was put on not at one of the big amphitheaters, the Globe or the Fortune, but by a boy's company at the
pricier Whitefriars. It therefore catered to a somewhat more
aristocratic or at least wealthier audience than attended the
amphitheaters, and the play may reflect gentlemanly disdain for
the tedious business of marriage upon which the middling sort
was expending so much energy. Significantly, the play's hero,
the aristocratic Dauphine, is never overpowered by desire for a
woman in a way that would make him vulnerable to a marriage
plot. Coolly self-contained, he incites desire in the Collegians,
but himself displays little passion, except a passion for his
uncle's money. Clearly, a heterosexual "companionate" marriage
is not the telos of his life; and in the Otters such a marriage is
roundly parodied. Moreover, as we have seen, what most fright-
ens Morose is an alliance with a "wife," at least an alliance
involving more than the appropriation of her economic or reproductive assets, since wives are associated in this play with noise,
motion, excessive spending, and the dethroning of men from
positions of patriarchal authority.[12] Dauphine's gentlemen companions seem more interested in women than he does; but these
rakes do not seem to be husbands, and Truewit is described as
having an "ingle" at home and a "mistress" abroad. Heterosexuality outside of marriage, coupled with various homoerotic
alliances, seem the norm within this social group. If Protestant
doctrine and the emerging middle class were giving new prominence to marriage as the "natural" center of men's and
women's emotional and sexual lives, *Epicoene* parodies and cir-
cumvents this institution and its heterosexual channeling of
erotic energy.[13] It does not, of course, follow that either such
resistance to marriage or an embrace of homoerotic alliances
necessarily be coupled with misogyny. But in Jonson's play this

is not the case. *Epicoene* not only critiques marriage; it circulates a virulent brand of antifeminist polemic.

The end of this play, when Morose's "bride" is revealed to be a boy, is one of the many moments when the early modern theater seems to point self-consciously to its own mode of theatrical production. When the character playing Epicoene is revealed to be a "he," this discovery invites another recognition: that *all* the "she's" of this theatrical production are really "he's." In a literal sense, stage interactions in a transvestite theater are interactions between men. The question is what to make of that fact. Was this a theater that addressed itself primarily to men or promoted solely homoerotic desire? I think not, although many critics, including myself, have paid too little attention to the homoeroticism inhering in the early modern mode of theatrical production and in many of the scripts as well. In the largest sense men controlled this stage in that they wrote the plays and constituted the troupes that enacted them. But, as we have seen, many patrons were women, and stage fictions had to accommodate their presence, if only by offering patriarchal constructions of femininity to female spectators. Even a play as critical of women as I believe *Epicoene* to be, allows a privileged class of aristocratic women to look down in disdain at the vulgarity of the Collegians or Mrs Otter. Such women, wealthy enough to be at a boys' theater production, could have the pleasure of aligning with the wit of a Dauphine and defining their femininity *against* that of the "unnatural" Collegians. This is certainly not a "progressive" subject position for women to occupy, pitting, as it does, women against one another along class lines. My point is hardly that the playscripts simply offered women "liberating" role models or progressive ideologies of gender. Many dramas of the period are overtly misogynist; many represent women who have voice and agency solely as criminals. What I *do* want to argue, however, is that the female spectator was never forgotten, and that a great deal was at stake in the representation of gender on the Renaissance stage. Women figured prominently in worries about social disorder in the period; and, as we have seen, women at the theater were real presences and real sources of anxiety. This theater spent a lot of time denigrating certain female behaviors and promoting others, but the process of ideological interpellation and control was never perfectly achieved. Even – as I am about to argue – plays as recuperative as Shakespeare's fictions of crossdressing open some new space for female agency and interiority even as they try to contain female will and desire.

More complicated still is the issue of the erotic investments encouraged by this stage, in part because sexual orientation was not a principal category through which social identity was defined in the way we now take for granted (Smith 1991: 11). As Alan Bray has argued, in this period homosexuality was seen as a potential within everyone, not as a separate sexuality (Bray 1988: 16), and it was only in the nineteenth century that the word *homosexuality* came into use. Not in dispute, of course, is the existence of same-sex sexual encounters in the Renaissance, especially, for men, between partners of unequal status such as teachers and students, masters and apprentices. For women the picture is less clear, though as Henrietta Andreadis has pointed out, the absence of widespread comment on or prosecution of what we would now call lesbian eroticism does not mean same-sex female erotic desire did not exist or that, in the case of someone like Katherine Philips, it did not find concrete forms of expression, though not necessarily those forms constituting lesbian sexuality today (Andreadis 1989: 59–60). Perhaps for some people what we now call homosexual and heterosexual practices were not seen as incompatible – Truewit's easy movement between ingle and mistress suggests as much. Only the full emergence of bourgeois culture – with its "elevation" of heterosexual passion as one of the chief foundations and solaces of marriage – heralded the instantiation of compulsory heterosexuality and the hiving off of homoerotic practice as a separate sexuality, and a deviant one at that.

It appears to me that in the early modern period sexuality was less fully developed than gender as a site of social contestation, despite the legal prohibition of sodomitical practices. While there most definitely was a subordinated gender, it is not so easy to say there was a subordinated sexuality in a culture in which the very idea that one had "a" sexuality seems not to have been thinkable in a twentieth-century sense. This does not mean, however, that early modern culture did not exert pressure on the production and channeling of erotic energy, or that specific classes and genders did not have different and sometimes competing erotic investments. Recently, Valerie Traub has argued, and I agree with her, that the early modern stage was a place of special erotic volatility and that a heterosexist bias in some feminist criticism, including my own, has overlooked the way the stage occasioned male and female homoerotic, as well as heterosexual, desire (Traub, 1992: 91–116). Yet plays are not all the same. In what follows I want both to pay attention to the multiple modalities of desire mobilized by these scripts in a transvestite theater and also to pay attention to distinct differences in how particular plays privilege specific forms of erotic desire.

For example, some plays in the period, such as *Epicoene*, eschew "the marriage plot" and the explicit channeling of erotic energy into the culturally constructed container of heterosexual marriage. Other dramas, no matter how much they enact varieties of erotic play, end up pushing homoerotic attachments to the periphery and privileging heterosexual closure. In such cases the transvestite mode of theatrical production stands in potential contradiction to the dominant sexual ideology implied by the plot. These variations suggest that the theater was neither simply a "heterosexual" nor a "homoerotic" institution, but a site where there was considerable fluidity and multiplicity in the channeling of sexual energies. Yet constantly the plays and the institution *were* exerting pressure on the construction of sexuality, and often, I would argue, class tensions were played out through contesting erotic practices: i.e. through the critique and embrace of heterosexual companionate marriage, through the embrace, eschewal, or erasure of male friendships, female friendships, and the figures of the Ganymede, the catamite, and the sodomite. In short, while it is surely a mistake to read sexuality in the period in modern, post-Freudian terms, it is also a mistake to romanticize the period as one in which the unfettered experience of polymorphous desire reigned supreme.

I will explore some of these matters further as I turn now to a series of plays in which women disguise themselves as men, addressing first the question of whether these plays challenge women's subordinate place in the Renaissance gender hierarchy or whether they recuperate the threat posed by the crossdressed woman in the streets of London and in the symbolic economy of the period. Second, I will explore how these plays channel erotic energy into or away from the institution of heterosexual marriage. If *Epicoene* responds to the threat of urban women by caricaturing and ridiculing them and literally makes heterosexual marriage collapse in on itself by the device of the boy bride, is the same true for plays of *female* crossdressing? To start this inquiry I am going to look briefly at three Shakespearean comedies, beginning with *Twelfth Night*, which I consider to be the most recuperative in terms of gender ideology. Undoubtedly, the crossdressed Viola, the woman who can sing both high and low and who is loved by a woman *and* by a man, is a figure who can be read as questioning the notion of fixed sexual difference. For Catherine Belsey that blurring of sexual difference opens the liberating possibility of undoing all the structures of domination and exploitation premised on binary sexual oppositions (Belsey 1985b: 166–90). The play therefore seems susceptible to a radical reading. For Stephen Greenblatt, by contrast, Viola's sexual indeterminacy simply signifies the play's projection onto the crossdressed woman of the process of *male* individuation, a stage in "the male trajectory of identity" (1988: 66–93). For Greenblatt, the play thus echoes those Renaissance medical discourses of gender which largely erased the question of female subjectivity and rooted masculine privilege in the natural "fact" "that within differentiated individuals is a single structure, identifiably male" (1988: 93).

I wish to question both readings, first by probing just how thoroughly Viola's gender identity is ever made indeterminate and thereby made threatening *to the theater audience* (the subjects being interpellated by the play's fictions), and second by calling attention to the degree to which the political threat of female insurgency enters the text, not through Viola, the crossdressed woman, but through Olivia, a figure whose sexual and economic independence is ironically reined in *by means of* the crossdressed Viola. The play enacts, not a happy allegory of the natural differentiation of male from female through erotic friction, but the containment of gender and class insurgency and the valorization of the "good woman" as the one who has interiorized – whatever her clothing – her essential differences from, and subordinate relations to, the male.[14] Put another way, the play seems to me to applaud a crossdressed woman who does not aspire to the positions of power assigned men and to discipline a non-crossdressed woman who does.

Talk about androgyny, or about erasure of sexual determinacy, always centers in regard to this play on the figure of Viola. Yet the first thing to say about her crossdressing is that it is in no way adopted to protest gender inequities or to prove that "custom is an idiot." Viola adopts male dress as a practical means of survival in an alien environment and, perhaps, as a magical means of keeping alive a brother believed drowned and of delaying her own entry into the heterosexual arena until that brother returns. In short, for her, crossdressing is not so much a political act as a psychological haven, a holding place. Moreover, and this is a key point, from the time Viola first meets Orsino in I. iv there is no doubt in the audience's mind of her sexual attraction to Orsino or her properly "feminine" subjectivity. As she says as she undertakes to be Orsino's go-between with Olivia, "Whoe'er I woo, myself would be his wife" (I. iv. 42). She never wavers in that resolve even while selflessly undertaking the task of wooing Olivia in Orsino's name. The audience always knows that underneath the page's clothes is a "real" woman, one who despises her own disguise, "Disguise, I see thou art a wickedness" (II. ii. 27), and one who freely admits that she has neither the desire nor the aptitude to play the man's part in phallic swordplay. The whole telos of the dramatic narrative is to release this woman from the prison of her masculine attire and return her to her proper and natural position as wife.

Part of the larger ideological consequence of her portrayal, moreover, is to shift the markers of sexual difference inward, from the surface of the body and the apparel that clothes that body, to the interior being of the gendered subject. The play shows that while crossdressing can cause semiotic and sexual confusion, and therefore is to be shunned, it is not truly a problem for the social order if "the heart" is untouched, or, put another way, if not accompanied by the political desire for a redefinition of female rights and powers and a dismantling of the hierarchical gender system. Despite her masculine attire and the confusion it causes in Illyria, Viola's is a properly feminine subjectivity; and this fact recuperates the threat posed by her clothes and displaces the possibility she will permanently aspire to masculine privilege and prerogatives. It is fair to say, I think, that Viola's portrayal, along with that of certain other of Shakespeare's crossdressed heroines, marks one of the points of emergence of the feminine subject of the bourgeois era: a woman whose limited freedom is premised on the interiorization of gender difference and the "willing" acceptance of differential access to power and to cultural and economic assets.

Just as clearly, however, the play records the quite traditional comic disciplining of a woman who lacks such a properly gendered subjectivity. I am referring, of course, to Olivia whom I regard as the real threat to the hierarchical gender system in this text, Viola being but an *apparent* threat. As Greenblatt points out, Olivia is a woman of property, headstrong and initially intractable, at least to the desires of Orsino, the play's highest-ranking male figure, and having no discernible male relatives, except the disreputable Toby, to control her or her fortune (Greenblatt 1988: 69). At the beginning of the play she has decided to do without the world of men, and especially to do without Orsino. These are classic marks of unruliness. And in this play she is punished, comically but unmistakably, by being made to fall in love with the crossdressed Viola. Viola's disguise makes possible the playing out of several homoerotic scenarios. In desiring her, Olivia desires a man who is "really" a woman. And while Orsino overtly desires a woman, Olivia, he ends up marrying the "boy," Cesario–Viola, who has served him so faithfully and who, fortuitously, turns out to be "really" a girl. Officially, the play "corrects" the wandering course of Eros so that Jack gets Jill in the end, but I think the play is much less firmly committed to heterosexuality than to the resecuring of men's domination of women. This is the comedy in which, for example, the overtly homoerotic attachment of Antonio for Sebastian goes uncritiqued, in fact, seems to stand as an example of selfless friendship. If I am right, moreover, that Olivia is the play's real threat to patriarchal power, it is her independence that must be curbed; her household and her person that must be placed under the control of a man. In the process her passion for the disguised Viola is presented comically, as an example of the madness that has overtaken Illyria when women grow too independent and men too passive. It is a marker of "the unnatural" that time and destiny must correct. Unintentionally, Viola becomes the vehicle for rendering the unruly Olivia comic in the eyes of the audience much as in *Midsummer Night's Dream* Titania's union with an ass renders her comic. But in the end, despite her "mistakings," Olivia marries a man. The play even brings on stage a priest to testify to that fact. While, when she marries, Olivia does not know the real identity of her husband, the audience knows she has married Sebastian, a fellow good with a sword.

The treatment of Orsino, by contrast, is much less satirical. He, too, initially poses a threat to the Renaissance gender system by languidly abnegating his active role as masculine wooer and drowning in narcissistic self-love. Yet Orsino, while mocked by Feste, escapes humiliating punishments. His narcissism and potential effeminacy are displaced, respectively, on to Malvolio and Andrew Aguecheek who suffer fairly severe punishments for their follies. Orsino, seemingly protected by his rank and gender, does not suffer a similar fate but simply emerges from his claustrophobic house in act V and assumes his "rightful" position as governor of Illyria and future husband of Viola. The woman who would not listen to him has been made the object of laughter and married off to another. But while his own final union with Viola is a "proper" one that puts him in the correct masculine position of authority over a subordinate, it is not clear that this union has a solely heterosexual valence on his part. After all, it is as his young male retainer that Orsino has known and come to feel affection for his "lamb." And never does Viola return, visually, to her women's clothing at play's end. While the drama conservatively underwrites the mainten-ance of gender and class hierarchies, it plays fast and loose with the question of a hierarchy of sexual practices, at least for men. For women heterosexual marriage is the primary cultural *form* in which their gender subordination is enacted. For a woman to be outside that institution, especially when she controls eco-nomic assets, is a form of transgression that must be stopped. But for Orsino what is important is not the homoerotic or hetero-sexual nature of his desire so much as his maintenance of a position of superiority vis-à-vis either a wife or a male subordi-nate. Viola–Cesario, conveniently, stands for both.

The emphasis on the preservation of hierarchy is enacted in the text's treatment of class, as well. If unruly women and unmanly men are sources of anxiety needing correction, so are upstart crows. The class jumper Malvolio who dresses himself up in yellow stockings and cross-garters, affecting the dress of a courtly gallant, is savagely punished and humiliated, echoing the more comically managed humiliation of Olivia, the woman who at the beginning of the play jumped gender boundaries to assume control of her house and person and refused her "natural" role in the patriarchal marriage market. The play disciplines independent women like Olivia and upstart crows such as Malvolio and rewards the self-abnegation of a Viola. In the process, female crossdressing is stripped of nearly all of its subversive resonances in the culture at large. There is no doubt that the play flirts with "dangerous matter." Wearing clothes of the opposite sex invites every kind of sexual confusion and "mistaking," but the greatest threat to the gender system is not, I would argue, the potential collapse of biological difference through the figure of Viola, but the failure of other characters – namely, Orsino and Olivia – to assume culturally sanctioned positions of dominance and subordination assigned the two genders. Ironically, it is through the crossdressed Viola, with her properly "feminine" subjectivity, that these threats are removed and gender hierarchy reinscribed.

Not all the comedies are so recuperative. Portia's crossdressing is more disruptive than Viola's, for example, precisely because Portia's is not so stereotypically a feminine subjectivity. We first see her chafing at the power of a dead father's control over her, and when she adopts male dress, she proves herself more than competent to enter the masculine arena of the courtroom and to hold her own as an advocate in that arena. Her man's disguise is not a psychological refuge, but a vehicle for assuming power. Unlike those crossdressed heroines who faint at the sight of blood or cannot wield a sword, Portia seems able to play the man's part with conviction. Her actions hardly dismantle the gender system; but they do reveal that masculine prerogatives are based on custom, not nature, since a woman can indeed successfully assume masculine positions of authority.[15] Portia's actions, however, are not aimed at letting her occupy a man's place indefinitely, but at making her place as a woman in patriarchy more bearable. She uses her disguise as Balthazar, not only to rescue Antonio from death, but to intervene in the male/male friendship of her husband and Antonio and to gain control over her sexuality and to set the terms for its use in marriage. By the ring trick she gains the right not to sleep with her husband, but by and with herself. In a play which insists on the patriarchal authority of fathers to dispose of daughters and husbands to govern wives, Portia's ability – through her impersonation of a man – to remain a married virgin and to set the terms for the loss of that state, is a remarkable feat, as is her ability to guide Bassanio's choice of the correct casket without violating the letter of her father's will.

The incipient subversiveness of this representation – a subversiveness registered still in those modern critical readings of her which stress her manipulative, castrating qualities (Berger 1981: 155–62) – is not unrelated to the fact that this is the most mercantile of Shakespeare's comedies in its preoccupations. At one level its ideological project is the reconciliation of landed and commercial wealth, a mediation between feudal and proto-capitalist economic systems (Cohen 1985: 195–211). But the mediation of class conflict through the trope of marriage in this instance cuts against the patriarchal gender system. By feminizing the gracious world of landed wealth and masculinizing the commercial world of Venice and by making the latter ill and unable to cure itself, Shakespeare created a fictional structure in which the ideology of male dominance breaks down. The woman is the only source of secure wealth, the only person capable in the courtroom of successfully playing the man's part and ousting the alien intruder. Portia may be "merely" an exception to her culture's patriarchal assumptions, but she, like Elizabeth, is an exception that has continued to provoke uneasiness. In every way she is a potentially unruly woman who avoids being marked as such by outward compliance with patriarchal culture's most basic requirements: namely, that a woman first obey her father and then submit to a marriage of his contriving. But if, as I have argued in regard to *Twelfth Night*, marriage is the chief cultural instrument of an adult woman's subordination, in this text it is not clear that marriage *will* in actuality subordinate Portia to Bassanio. In fact, perhaps most striking is her implicit demand that he subordinate his attachment to Antonio to his attachment to her. In this play the woman seems to insist that marriage bonds have priority for her husband, as well as herself, over other affective and social bonds, including Sebastian's longstanding friendship with Antonio. If this homoerotic attachment is neither criminalized nor stigmatized, it is, nonetheless, pushed to the margins by Portia's insistence on the primacy of the wedlock union.

Of course, it should be noted that not all the *critical* uneasiness about Portia has its roots in patriarchal anxiety about strong and clever women. Portia also voices unmistakably racist views in her wish that Morocco and "all of his complexion" (IV. vii.

117

79) fail in their attempts to woo her. And she is fully complicit with the Venetian state in its effective destruction of the alien, Shylock's, identity and in its appropriation of his property. In short, while Portia seizes power for herself within and against a patriarchal society, she does so at the expense of, rather than in alliance with, other marginalized figures.

More complex still is *As You Like It* which explicitly invites, through its epilogue, a consideration of how secure even the most recuperative representations of crossdressing can be in a theater in which male actors regularly played women's roles. Rosalind's crossdressing, of course, occurs in the holiday context of the pastoral forest, and, as Natalie Davis has argued, holiday inversions of order can spur social change or, in other instances, merely reconfirm the existing order (Davis 1978: 153–4). The representation of Rosalind's holiday humor has the primary effect, I think, of confirming the gender system and perfecting, rather than dismantling, it by making a space for mutuality within relations of dominance (Novy 1984: 21–44). Temporarily lording it over Orlando, teaching him how to woo and appointing the times of his coming and going, she *could* be a threatening figure did she not constantly, contrapuntally, reveal herself to the audience as the not-man, as in actuality a lovesick maid whose love "hath an unknown bottom, like the bay of Portugal" (IV. ii. 208), and who faints at the sight of blood. Crucially, like Viola, Rosalind retains a properly feminine subjectivity. As she says: "dost thou think, though I am caparison'd like a man, I have a doublet and hose in my disposition?" (III. ii. 194–6). As Annette Kuhn has argued, in certain circumstances crossdressing intensifies, rather than blurs, sexual difference, sometimes by calling attention to the woman's inability to perform the masculine roles signified by her dress (Kuhn 1985: 48–73, esp. 55–7). Rosalind's fainting constitutes such a reminder, endearing her to generations of readers for her true "womanliness." Moreover the movement of the narrative is toward that long delayed moment of disclosure, orchestrated so elaborately in act V, when the heroine will doff her masculine attire and the saucy games of youth and accept the position of wife, when her biological identity, her gender identity, and the semiotics of dress will coincide.

Yet where this account of the consequences of Rosalind's crossdressing becomes too simple is when we consider the

particular *way* in which Rosalind plays with her disguise. Somewhat like Portia, Rosalind uses her disguise to redefine in a
limited way the position of woman in patriarchy. The unusual
part of her behavior is that it is versions of her self – rather,
cultural constructions of the female self – which she performs
for Orlando while in her male disguise, playing out, for
example, the role of fickle Petrarchan lady and showing how
tedious it would be as a paradigm for daily behavior rather
than simply an idealization carved on a tree. Marianne Doane
has argued that "masquerade," the self-conscious staging,
parody, exaggeration of cultural constructions of self, offers
women an option between simple identification with male selves
– which is how she reads the meaning of crossdressing – or
simple inscription within patriarchal constructions of the feminine (Doane 1982: 74–89). The figure of Rosalind, dressed as a
boy, engages, I would argue, in playful masquerade as in playing Rosalind for Orlando she acts out the parts scripted for
women by her culture. Doing so does not put Rosalind outside
patriarchy, but it reveals the constructed nature of patriarchy's
representations of the feminine and shows a woman manipulating those representations in her own interest, theatricalizing for
her own purposes what is assumed to be innate, teaching her
future mate how to get beyond certain ideologies of gender to
more enabling ones.

Moreover, this play, more than other Shakespearean comedies,
deliberately calls attention to the destabilizing fact that it is boy
actors playing the roles of all the women in the play, including
Rosalind. There is a permanent gap on the stage between the at
least incipiently masculine identity of the boy actors and their
appropriation of the "grace,/Voice, gait, and action of a gentlewoman" – to borrow a definition of the actor's task from the
job assigned the Page in the Induction to *The Taming of the Shrew*
(Ind. 131–2). I agree with Kathleen McLuskie that at some level
boy actors playing women must simply have been accepted in
performance as a convention (McLuskie 1987: 120–30). Otherwise, there would have been little audience involvement with
those aspects of the plays based on the representation of heterosexual desire. It is also true, as McLuskie and others suggest,
that the convention of the boy actor playing a girl can, at any
moment, be unmasked *as* a convention and the reality that the
fictional woman is played by a boy can be revealed. Such

moments not only further the potential for the homoerotic attraction of male audience members to the boy actor, but also resonate with those moments of the plays based on the representation of homoerotic desire. One of those moments occurs at the end of *As You Like It*. The play has achieved closure in part by reinscribing everyone into his or her "proper" social position. The duke is now again a duke and not a forest outlaw, Rosalind is now Rosalind and not Ganymede, and so forth. But when in the epilogue the character playing Rosalind reveals she is played by a boy, the neat convergence of biological sex and culturally constructed gender is once more severed. If a boy can so successfully personate the voice, gait, and manner of a woman, how stable are those boundaries separating one sexual kind from another, and so, how secure are those powers and privileges assigned to the hierarchically superior sex which depends upon notions of difference to justify its dominance?[16]

The epilogue playfully invites this question, just as it invites the question of where the erotic energy between the actors, the characters, and audience is flowing. Progressively this text has narrowed the range of erotic possibilities the play has mobilized in the direction of heterosexual coupling. For example, it has displaced the same-sex bonds between Rosalind and Celia with heterosexual unions; it has muted the homoerotic implications of Rosalind's assumption of the name of Ganymede by having Rosalind and Orlando so firmly committed to the heterosexual other; and, as with Olivia, it has corrected Phoebe's "mistake" in loving a man who is "really" a woman. The epilogue opens up again what has been gradually foreclosed. In the epilogue the character Rosalind enjoins the men and the women of the audience to have the "play" between them be pleasurable. At the same time, revealing himself as a male actor, the figure playing Rosalind says that *if* he were a woman (which is how by his dress he appears), he would kiss all the men who pleased him. In one gesture, this femininely clad man reaches out, erotically, to the men of the audience as a woman in supposition and as a man in actuality. In such both/and, rather than either/or, situations, there is revealed something of the contradictory nature of the theater as a site of ideological production. At one and the same time it can put in play recuperative fables of crossdressing that reinscribe sexual difference, gender hierarchy, and heterosexual marriage, and it can make visible on the level of theatrical practice the contamination of sexual kinds and the multiplication of erotic possibility.

Whatever else may be said by way of generalization about Shakespeare's comedies of female crossdressing, they all eventually commit their heroines to the institution of marriage (Rose 1988: 37). This fact marks the limits of their challenge to patriarchal ideology. To varying degrees these dramas reveal the constructedness of gender ideology and to some extent rewrite and enlarge woman's place in the patriarchal order, but they do not allow a marriageable woman to remain unmarried. And since marriage, even a "companionate one," placed women in political and economic subordination to their husbands, to make marriage the telos of woman's existence effectively confirmed her permanent subordination and often, in the plays, the loosening of her bonds with other women. The last play I want to examine, Middleton and Dekker's *The Roaring Girl*, is a different kettle of fish. The one thing it shares with *Epicoene* is a critique of marriage. But while *Epicoene* critiques marriage because it might tie men to women who would assert agency by talking, moving outside the home, and buying things, *The Roaring Girl* critiques marriage precisely because it gives men too much power over women. In the figure of Moll Frith we encounter a crossdressed woman who embodies a more radical assault than do Shakespeare's heroines on the hierarchical gender system and the material injustices which, in conjunction with other social practices, it spawned. In addition, the play is more forthright than most in exploring the links between women's political subordination and the channeling of her erotic desire into heterosexual marriage.

The play is based on an actual London woman's life and is traversed by discourses of social protest not found in most of the plays I have so far examined. First, as Mary Beth Rose has argued, this play is unusual in presenting us with a woman who does not use male dress *as a disguise* (Rose 1988: 64–5). She does not don male apparel to escape from danger or to pursue a husband. In this she differs from Mary, the hero's love interest in the drama, who in the first act puts on the clothes of a seamstress to approach her lover secretly. Her disguise (though not one of crossdressing), gives Mary a certain freedom, but its sole purpose is to enable her, ultimately, to become a wife. By contrast, Moll adopts male dress deliberately and publicly; and she uses it to signal her freedom from the traditional positions assigned a woman in her culture. As she says to the young hero:

> I have no humour to marry, I love to lie o' both sides o'th'bed myself, and again o'th'other side; a wife you know ought to be obedient, but I fear me I am too headstrong to obey, therefore I'll ne'er go about it. I love you so well, sir, for your good will I'd be loath you should repent your bargain after, and therefore we'll ne'er come together at first. I have the head now of myself, and am man enough for a woman; marriage is but a chopping and changing, where a maiden loses one head and has a worse i'th'place.[17]

> (II. ii. 36–44)

The issue is control. Refusing a male head, Moll retains a freedom not usually associated with the woman's place. Dressed as a woman she enters the merchants' shops; dressed as a man she fights with Laxton at Gray's Inn Fields; and at the end of the play she moves easily among the rogues and "canters" of the London underworld. In short, not immured within a domestic role within the house, she retains her freedom to move about.

Of course, a woman who thus contravenes the accepted conventions governing female dress – who smokes a pipe, carries a sword, bobs her hair, and dons French slops (see the frontispiece of the play for an illustration of such a subversive and disorderly woman) – invites being read as a whore, as a woman at the mercy of an ungovernable sexual appetite. Importantly, the play insists on Moll Frith's chastity. This can be read as a way of containing the subversiveness of her representation, of showing her accepting the central fact of the good woman's lot – i.e. that she not use her sexuality except in lawful marriage. Another way to read the insistence on chastity is to see it as an interruption of that discourse about women which equates a mannish independence with sexual promiscuity. In the play Moll is constantly read by the men around her as a potential bedmate, a sexual prize. Even Trapdoor, the servant hired to spy on Moll, assumes he can master her sexually, that, when "her breeches are off, she shall follow me" (I. ii. 223). Laxton, the gentleman rake, makes the same mistake, finding her mannish clothes sexually provocative, the gap between the semiotic signals of her dress and her well-known biological identity making her hidden body the more alluring. Tellingly, Moll both refuses Laxton's sexual advances and offers him a reading of some women's sexual promiscuity that is refreshingly economic in orientation. If the master narrative of the *Hic Mulier* tracts is that women's sexual looseness stems from their unnatural aspiration beyond their assigned place, that is, beyond the control of the male, Moll argues that women sleep around because they are poor. She may give us the best gloss on those women, dressed as men, who were hauled before the Aldermen's Court and accused of "lewd" behavior. To Laxton Moll says:

> In thee I defy all men, their worst hates,
> And their best flatteries, all their golden witchcrafts,
> With which they entangle the poor spirits of fools.
> Distressed needlewomen and trade-fallen wives,
> Fish that must needs bite or themselves be bitten,
> Such hungry things as these may soon be took
> With a worm fastened on a golden hook:
> Those are the lecher's food, his prey, he watches
> For quarrelling wedlocks, and poor shifting sisters,
> 'Tis the best fish he takes: but why, good fisherman,
> Am I thought meat for you, that never yet
> Had angling rod cast towards me? 'cause, you'll say,
> I'm given to sport, I'm often merry, jest:
> Had mirth no kindred in the world but lust?
>
> (III. i. 90–103)

Rather than accepting that it is women's nature which is to be endlessly debated and her person disciplined, Moll turns attention to the social realities which create conditions for the sale of sex and to the assumptions made by men about women.

But this does not mean Moll lacks erotic desire. In fact, the play insists on her desire, which makes more striking both her resistance to marriage and to extramarital encounters. Throughout the text Moll is linked to the playing of a particular musical instrument, the viol. As you recall, the original Moll Frith gained some of her considerable notoriety from playing a lute on the stage of the Fortune theater. As Linda Austern has shown, women playing musical instruments – usually the smaller stringed instruments or the virginals – were considered to be erotically stimulating, the combination of feminine beauty and musical concord acting together, siren-like, to rouse men to uncontrollable passion (Austern 1989: 427). Consequently, women, if they played, were to do so in private, for their own recreation or for the delight of family and husband, and never in public. Moll Frith was thus transgressive to play her lute on the public stage. Moll Cutpurse is even more transgressive in that her instrument is not the lute, able to be tucked decorously beneath the breast, but the viol, played, manlike, with legs akimbo. In II. ii Moll enters with a porter bearing a viol on his back, taking it to her chamber. In act IV, when Sebastian has Mary, disguised now as a boy, in his father's chamber, Sebastian urges Moll to "here take this viol, run upon the guts,/And end thy quarrel singing" (IV. i. 79–80). Moll complies, and there follows a great deal of double-edged banter about Moll's skills as a musician, whether or not she initiates the taking up of a gentleman's "instrument," whether or not, as some "close" women would say, there is something unmannerly in her playing upon such an instrument. At the climax of this jesting, Moll says she doesn't care what other women say. When they accuse her of lewdness, she falls asleep and dreams. Then, in two songs, she recounts her dreams, which turn out to be about two "loose" women, one of whom gads about London "laying out the money" and coming home "with never a penny," the other who sleeps with a man from the navy while her husband is in prison. These "dreams" seem to function, doubly, as angry indictments of the hypocritical "dames" who would call Moll whore and yet seize sexual pleasure for themselves, and as wishful projections of a longed-for freedom for herself. Moll seems to acknowledge the latter reading when, the songs over, she says "Hang up the viol now, sir: all this while I was in a dream, one shall lie rudely then; but being awake, I keep my legs together" (IV. i. 127–9).

This encounter is riveting to me for the way it acknowledges, insists upon, female erotic desire, while making clear the cultural imperatives that operate to shape, channel, and control that eroticism. It is not clear exactly what *kind* of erotic alliances and practices Moll would find most pleasurable. Others, mostly enemies or critics, accuse her of sexual "doubleness." Sir Alexander Wengrave, for example, accuses her of being a monster, presumably an hermaphrodite who "casts two shadows" (I. ii. 132) and has two "trinkets" in her breeches. The fact Moll is

personated by a boy actor, of course, gives this suggestion purchase at the level of the dramatic presentation. Laxton also
comments that as man/woman Moll "might first cuckold the
husband and then make him do as much for the wife" (II. i.
192–3). He also describes Moll as "slipping from one company
to another like a fat eel between a Dutchman's fingers" (II. i.
188–9). This image of Moll's slippery doubleness, which allows
her to slip from one place to another, one class group to another,
might, it is hinted, extend to her sexual practices as well. Moll
herself, when refusing Sebastian's marriage proposal, says "I
love to lie on both sides of the bed myself," meaning that
she likes her independence; perhaps that she likes a certain
unspecified variety in sexual partners and practices; perhaps
that she likes to be her own chief source of erotic pleasure.

The play is not explicit about what we would now call Moll's
sexual orientation. It insinuates a multiplicity of possibilities,
and this multiplicity is in part what makes her both alluring and
dangerous. What is quite explicit is Moll's refusal to engage in
heterosexual sex on the terms her society sets for her. Except
in dreams, Moll cannot be a free sexual subject and escape being
called a whore. She is allowed, of course, to enter a heterosexual
marriage, but while Moll is desired and has desire, is erotic
subject as well as object, she will not marry to give her desire
expression. Her reasons are explicitly political. As she says to
Sebastian: "marriage is but a chopping and changing, where a
maiden loses one head and has a worse i'th'place" (I. ii. 43–4).
Refusing woman's position of subordination in patriarchal marriage, she equally refuses extramarital encounters with the brag-
garts Laxton and Trapdoor who could make her simply a sexual
conquest. She physically assaults and humiliates both of them
when they try to "board" her in this fashion. Yet Moll never
denies her sexuality. She has and acknowledges her sexual
dreams; she has and acknowledges her "instrument," that viol
with which she is so insistently linked. In fact, at play's end,
joking with Sir Alexander Wengrave, now her friend, Moll says:
"And you can cuck me, spare not:/Hang up my viol by me,
and I care not" (V. ii. 253–4). She can imagine enduring public
humiliation for female transgression as long as she can defiantly
exhibit her viol, sign of the sexual being she is. It is not stretch-
ing, I think, to argue that through her one starkly realizes that
the culturally sanctioned ways for woman to express erotic

desire may exact too high a price to be employed. To be an object of desire may be flattering, to be married may be the culturally inscribed telos of woman's existence, but for Moll there seems to be no way, outside of dream and solitary prick-song, to gratify Eros without enduring an unendurable subordination and exploitation. Yet in her jaunty defiance she makes us feel she is no victim, that keeping her legs together outside of dreams, and retaining her mighty voice, her outlandish dress and her mobility, are preferable to any other bargain she might have struck with her culture.

Importantly, besides being a critic of patriarchal marriage, Moll is also associated with the righting of a great variety of other social ills. In act V she is explicitly associated with Long Meg of Westminster, a colorful character described in Renaissance ballads and a lost play and who embodied lower-class resistance to established authority and for much of her life protested against the injustices of patriarchal marriage.[18] For the last two acts of *The Roaring Girl*, Moll, like Meg of Westminster, and a bit like a Lady Skimington, protests against and remedies various social injustices. It is she who, for example, rescues Jack Dapper from the law when his father would have him unjustly incarcerated, proclaiming "If any gentleman be in scrivener's bands/Send but for Moll, she'll bail him by these hands" (III. iii. 216–17). She also is instrumental in interrupting the tyrannous plans of Sebastian's father to keep his son, for economic reasons, from marrying Mary Fitz-Allard. And she is the one who unmasks the knavery of the two lowlife characters, Tearcat and Trapdoor, who are impersonating wounded soldiers and in that guise fleecing people for alms money. Further, she makes a thief promise to return a purse he had filched from one of her friends during a new play at the Swan theater. In short, Moll is a social reformer, though it is not always perfectly clear that she embodies a consistent social philosophy or class–gender position. For example, seeing marriage as a strait-jacket for herself, she nevertheless promotes it for Mary Fitz-Allard and other women. No thief, she nevertheless knows all the lowlife types of London and knows their canting jargon, their thieving tricks. Paradoxically she both reproves criminals and critiques the social system that produces their criminality. In modern terms, she functions at once as liberal reformer and radical revolutionary.

Obviously, contradictions surround the figure of Moll, the woman who touches pitch and is not defiled. Middleton and Dekker have attempted to decriminalize her, to present her as neither thief nor whore, to make her an exception to society's rules concerning women's behavior but not a fundamental threat to the gender system. But her portrayal is not entirely innocuous and sanitized. It partakes of discursive traditions of social protest, including protest against Renaissance patriarchal marriage and women's position within such marriages, that contradict the tendency simply to construct her as an eccentric "exception." In the final moments of the play, asked when she will marry, Moll replies:

> I'll tell you when i' faith:
> When you shall hear
> Gallants void from sergeants' fear,
> Honesty and truth unslandered,
> Woman manned but never pandered
> Cheaters booted but not coached,
> Vassals older ere they're broached,
> If my mind be then not varied,
> Next day following I'll be married.
> (V. ii. 216–24)

Enigmatic, like the fool's prophecy in *Lear*, Moll's prophecy is clear in its utopian aspirations, clear in making the ending of women's oppression a central part of a more encompassing utopian vision of social reform. More than most plays of the period, *The Roaring Girl* uses the image of the crossdressed woman to defy expectations about woman's nature and to protest the injustices caused by the gender system.[19] And if comedy demands a marriage, it gets the marriage of Mary Fitz-Allard and Sebastian, but not the marriage of Moll.

In summary, then, one can paint only a very complicated picture of what crossdressing and its theatrical representation "meant" in early modern England. This form of theatricality, both as social practice and as stage convention, had no single or fixed meaning precisely because it was a counter in ongoing ideological struggles, a practice whose meaning was under contest. Often, on the stage, the more radical social and political implications of female crossdressing were contained. Rather than blurring gender difference or challenging male domination

and exploitation of women, female crossdressing could strength-
en notions of difference by stressing what the disguised woman
could not do, or by emphasizing those feelings held to constitute
a "true" female subjectivity. While some plots *do* reveal women
successfully wielding male power and male authority, they
usually end with the female's willing doffing of male clothes
and, presumably, male prerogatives. Such plots serve the purpose of recuperating threats to the gender system, sometimes
by ameliorating the worst aspects of that system and opening a
greater space for woman's speech and action.

Yet this recuperation is never perfectly achieved. In a few
plays, such as *Roaring Girl*, the resistance to patriarchy and its
marriage customs is clear and sweeping; in others, such as
Merchant of Venice, the heroine achieves a significant rewriting
of her position within patriarchy even as she takes up the role of
wife. Still other dramas, simply by having women successfully
play male roles, however temporarily, or by making women's
roles the objects of self-conscious masquerade, put in question
the naturalness, the inevitability, of dominant constructions of
men's and women's natures and positions within gender hierarchies. Moreover, even as the comic genre in which crossdressing motifs most often occur worked to channel erotic energy
into heterosexual marriage, crossdressing plots often play on the
"mistakings" that temporarily allow man to love man, woman
to love woman. And at some level the fact that boy actors
played women's parts kept in play a homoerotic counterpoint
to the heterosexual telos of many of the comedic plots. In short,
the theater – comprised both of material practices of production
and spectatorship, as well as of dramatic scripts and conventions
– was uniquely positioned to embody many of the most fundamental tensions and contradictions of the period. This is no less
true in matters of gender and sexuality than in matters of class
conflict, monarchical legitimacy, or the relationship of England
to the New World. What is interesting to me is that, like Portia,
the theater so often embraced a seemingly conservative path
while actually undermining the very orthodoxies it promulgated.

But it is time now to turn away from the overt theatricality of
the crossdresser, often a woman, to the more covert theatricality
of the culture's most important figure, the monarch, who, unsur-
prisingly, was usually a man.

6

KINGS AND PRETENDERS
Monarchical theatricality in the Shakespearean history play

Most of the time when women characters crossdress in Shakespeare's comedies, the audience is aware they are doing it. These characters, that is, transform themselves before spectators who know who "really" lurks beneath the doublet and hose. The relations of power and knowledge that obtain at such moments are important. Rosalind may fool Orlando and for a time gain power to speak her mind with unusual freedom, but the audience is not fooled. Within the frame of the fiction, we know that this is a woman playing at being a man; and typically the comedies end with an unveiling in which what "we" know is revealed to everyone on stage as well. As a rule, then, it might be said that crossdressed women in comedy temporarily achieve unusual power and freedom on condition that the audience know in advance that theirs is "licensed foolery," performed before unmystified beholders. Moreover, part of the theatrical pleasure for the spectator lies in seeing how well or badly or comically a "woman" performs the role of masculinity. In short, the women characters display theatrical prowess under carefully controlled conditions. In real life, the crossdresser was more threatening and more stigmatized.

In the Shakespearean history play crossdressing is not the primary form theatricality takes, nor are displays of theatricality primarily contained within the frame of festive foolery. Rather, the liminal and dangerous conditions of civil war afford the primary arena in which identities seem to become detached from social place and social function and susceptible to dangerous and disruptive manipulation. And it is never clear that the transgressive threat posed by theatricality can be contained, that a silver-tongued pretender or an ambitious woman with demonic powers may not take over or undermine the state. Obviously, it is the figure of the king upon whom anxiety about the counterfeitability of identity is most intensely focused. I am going to argue, however, that there is a considerable difference between how theatricality is represented as a threat to identity and social stability in the three plays dealing with the reign of Henry VI and in the plays dealing primarily with Bolingbroke and his son. The difference can be represented a number of ways, but it has centrally to do with whether or not theatrical practice is represented as an external threat *to* monarchy or as constitutive *of* monarchy. Ultimately, that formulation proves too simple, however, since the difference I am exploring is relative, not absolute, and because it is not *only* monarchy that becomes in some profound sense performative rather than essential in the course of these plays, but also many other forms of social identity as well. It is the plays dealing with Bolingbroke and his son, however, that most insistently mark their modernity by demonstrating the inseparability of theatricality from social being.

THE *HENRY VI* PLAYS AND DEMONIZED THEATRICALITY

Phyllis Rackin has brilliantly shown how, in the first tetralogy, Shakespeare represents monarchical legitimacy as continually threatened by female sexual will (Rackin 1990: 158–61). Claims to the throne are repeatedly made by reciting genealogies often as tedious as the recitation of "begats" in the Bible. But these recitations of male lineage – beginning typically with Edward III, moving to an enumeration of his seven sons, and then to an elaboration of the claims to the throne of the offspring of one of these sons – are crucial in a feudal world in which legitimacy descends through a blood line. One way to disrupt the purity of these lines is through female sexual errancy. Charges of bastardy figure prominently in attempts to delegitimate rival contenders to the throne. Richard III, for example, calls Edward's two sons "those bastards in the Tower" (*Richard III* IV. ii. 75), and the women of the Henry VI plays, in particular, are often depicted as willful, unwomanly, and beyond the control of husbands or fathers. Frequently, the taint of the unnatural clings to them – Joan is said to be "an Amazon" (*1 Henry VI* I. ii. 104); Margaret is accused of possessing "a tiger's heart" (*3 Henry VI* I. iv. 137); Eleanor is depicted as the intimate of conjurers and witches (*2 Henry VI* I. iv).

The sexual promiscuity supposedly consequent upon their "unnatural" forwardness is insinuated in myriad ways. The treatment of Joan de Pucelle is exemplary. The English constantly imply that the maid with the sword is really a puzzel or drab (*1 Henry VI* I. iv. 107), the Dauphin's trull (II. ii. 28). When Bedford asks: "A maid? and be so martial?" (II. i. 21), he voices everyone's assumption: that Joan's aggressiveness means she cannot be (1) properly feminine, (2) properly subservient, and (3) properly chaste.[1] Similarly, Margaret of Anjou, the strong-willed woman who goes to the battlefield to defend her son's right to the throne, is depicted as enamoured of Suffolk, the noble who brought her from France. When he is beheaded, Margaret (in one of the more grotesque moments in the first tetralogy) carries Suffolk's severed head about the court until Henry remarks that should he himself die, Margaret would not mourn him so dearly (*2 Henry VI* IV. iv. 21–4). In the disordered world of civil war, blame for the uncertainty about who is really the king often comes to rest with women who – pictured as monsters of desire and aggression – both undermine the purity of blood lines by their sexual appetites and increase social instability by their ambition.

But it is not *only* female sexual will that threatens social stability and monarchical legitimacy in these plays. Other disruptive figures people the play's landscape – figures such as Jack Cade, Simpcox, and Horner and his apprentice, Peter. Though sharply etched, many of these figures hold the stage only briefly, but their presence suggests that the causes and consequences of social disorder encompass more than gender insurgency, central though that is. The relationship between such figures and the disruptive women is established primarily by means of the significant scene juxtapositions characteristic of the episodic dramaturgy of these plays (Rose 1972: 127–35), and by the insistent deployment of antitheatrical discourse to weld together their various modes of transgression.

For illustration, I want to concentrate for a moment on Part 2. This play is characterized by a number of short, narratively disconnected episodes. Only cumulatively do they acquire symbolic power, eventually making visible the logic by which

Shakespeare represents Henry's crisis of monarchical authority and his country's descent into civil war. Strikingly, the more the crowned king proves weak and out of love with his greatness, the more insistently his England becomes peopled with imposters, egotistical and theatrical overreachers, and aspiring, deceptive women. Sanctioned rites such as coronations and trials of single combat become subject to parody, while illegitimate forms of theatrical practice, such as conjuration, flourish. "Minor" characters, often the women and the lower-class figures who hover so vividly on the margins of the text, make manifest an anxiety about theatricality that ultimately finds its apogee in the monstrous figure of Richard III.

Consider, for example, Saunder Simpcox. He appears just once, but memorably, in act II of Part 2. He is the tetralogy's most blatant example of a simple charlatan, someone who uses deception to gain power for himself. His trickery depends on belief in religious miracles. At the shrine of St Albans he pretends to have gained his eyesight after a life of blindness. The story was included in John Foxe's *Acts and Monuments* as an example of the clergy's chicanery and Duke Humphrey's prudence, a man described by Foxe as "meek and gentle, loving the Commonwealth, a supporter of the poor commons" (Foxe 1877: 712). Shakespeare retains much of the anticlerical force of Foxe in that the Simpcox episode is preceded by an angry exchange of threats and insults between Gloucester, the Protector, and Cardinal Beaufort, Bishop of Winchester. While there is no direct implication that Winchester stagemanaged Simpcox's hoax, the association of Simpcox with St Albans' shrine forges a link between his actions and deceptive Catholic practices. Much as in *The Whore of Babylon*, a binary is established between theatrical deceit and plaindealing, with Winchester/Simpcox and the clear-eyed Duke Humphrey as their respective embodiments.

In structure the scene works to displace the false miracle of St Albans' shrine with a spectacle of truth and justice engineered by the good duke. The episode opens spectacularly when someone enters "crying 'A miracle!' " (S.D. after II. i. 56). A procession soon follows involving what must be a significant number of people. The stage directions read: "Enter the Mayor of Saint Albons and his Brethren, [with music,] bearing the man [Simpcox] between two in a chair, [Simpcox's Wife and others following]" (S.D. after II. i. 65). The citizenry has been taken in by Simpcox and caught up in the celebration of the miraculous recovery of his eyesight. Of course, the gullible king never questions the report, but exclaims: "Now God be prais'd, that to believing souls/Gives light in darkness, comfort in despair!" (II. i. 64–5). More skeptical, Gloucester questions Simpcox, trapping him into naming the colors of a cloak and gown despite the fact that he could not possibly have done so had he really been blind his whole life. The episode ends when Gloucester calls in the beadles to whip Simpcox, who also claims to be lame, in order to "cure" his disability. Force has its effect: "After the Beadle hath hit him once, he leaps over the stool and runs away: and they follow and cry, 'A miracle!'" (S.D. after II. i. 150). In short, Gloucester and the law perform the "miracle" of revealing chicanery while discrediting the false miracle by which the imposture had deceived the mayor, the king, and a considerable number of townspeople.

There is, of course, a sad as well as a funny side to this episode. The wife, threatened with punishment, pleads that she and her husband "did it for pure need" (II. i. 154), perhaps the only plausible claim she makes. Poverty and need are realities to which the king and his officers seem to have little time to attend. And neither does the play, though glimpses of economic injustice and hardship surface again later in Cade's call for cheaper food and drink and a commonwealth where "All the realm shall be in common" (IV. ii. 68). In the main, however, Simpcox functions not to indict, but to be indicted. He represents the charlatanry and deception springing up, Hydra-headed, in the absence of a powerful authority at the head of the state. As in the antitheatrical tracts, the victims of cultural chaos are often written as its primary instigators.

The topoi and conventions of antitheatrical discourse repeatedly provide a language by which to render England's condition intelligible. The gullible, guileless king has, as the son of Henry V, a strong, if not impregnable claim to the throne, but he is powerless to subdue or rein in the dangerously theatrical energies of his enemies. Throughout the plays involving Henry, a series of powerful nobles attempt to do for him what he cannot do for himself. Talbot tries to save France; Gloucester attempts to smash the power of the prelates; Suffolk, Somerset, and a host of other champions lead his men in the battles from which

Henry himself prefers to be absent. But like mushrooms the pretenders and charlatans proliferate. Simpcox is just part of a chain of figures in *2 Henry VI* who, beginning with Eleanor Cobham and ending with Cade, dress themselves in borrowed robes and aspire to be what they are not. Repeatedly, these figures are connected with sedition, with the demonic, and with the unnatural. The tropes and organizing preoccupations of the antitheatrical tradition thus permeate the representation of social danger in these texts. Poor Simpcox, made to count as a sign of the pernicious effects of clerical deceit, is but one instance of this phenomenon.

Eleanor Cobham is a more significant figure. In the first scene of Part 1 Winchester accuses Gloucester of being "in awe" of his wife (I. i. 39), and she becomes the vehicle through which the cardinal is able to bring down his rival. Eleanor is presented as a theatrical overreacher. Early in Part 2 she recounts a dream to her husband:

> Methought I sate in seat of majesty
> In the cathedral church of Westminster,
> And in that chair where kings and queens were crown'd,
> Where Henry and Dame Margaret kneel'd to me,
> And on my head did set the diadem.
>
> (I. ii. 36–40)

Gloucester is appalled at her presumption, but this does not stop Eleanor from exclaiming to herself that "being a woman, I will not be slack/To play my part in Fortune's pageant" (I. ii. 66–7). She imagines herself, not as defined by her role as the Protector's wife, but as an actor seizing whatever role Fortune gives her the opportunity to play. Her ambitions are reflected in her clothes. In the next scene the queen complains bitterly that Eleanor

> sweeps it through the court with troops of ladies,
> More like an empress than Duke Humphrey's wife.
> Strangers in court do take her for the Queen.
> She bears a duke's revenues on her back,
> And in her heart she scorns our poverty.
> Shall I not live to be aveng'd on her?
> Contemptuous base-born callot as she is,
> She vaunted 'mongst her minions t' other day,

134

The very train of her worst wearing gown
Was better worth than all my father's lands,
Till Suffolk gave two dukedoms for his daughter.

(I. iii. 77–87)

Not a gender crossdresser, Eleanor is a class crossdresser, someone who wears on her back the borrowed robes of monarchy itself. Yet her violations of status hierarchies, reflected in her dress, are paralleled by her gender insubordination. Refusing to obey her husband's commands that she be content with her status as his wife, she defies him and calls in Margery Jordan, the witch, and Roger Bolingbrook, the conjurer, to give her information about the king and other prominent members of the court that might further her ambitious plans.

The association of Eleanor with witchcraft links her to that other overreaching woman, Joan of Arc, from Part 1, and provides the excuse for both of them to be punished, Joan by burning, and Eleanor by a shaming ritual and banishment (Hodgdon 1991: 61). Eleanor is literally demonized in the sense of being associated with demonic rituals of conjuration, and these are in turn the basis for an accusation of treason. Buckingham says to Henry that Eleanor and others have "practic'd dangerously against your state,/Dealing with witches and with conjurers,/Whom we have apprehended in the fact,/Raising up wicked spirits from under ground,/Demanding of King Henry's life and death,/And other of your Highness' Privy Council,/As more at large your Grace shall understand" (II. i. 167–73).

As Howard Dobin has shown, the riddling prophecies of witches and conjurers were often taken to be politically seditious and demonic in origin (1990: 105–33, 167–71). By connecting Eleanor with sedition, the play mobilizes specific ideologies of gender to voice its political anxieties. Eleanor is presented as the headstrong, unmasterable woman whose ambition takes her beyond the control of her husband and expresses itself first in the assumption of a sartorial splendour not befitting her station and second in the illicit connection with demonic powers. In her person Henry and the court find a scapegoat. The audience hears that Simpcox is to be whipped to Berwick, but the audience actually sees Eleanor in her white sheet, barefoot, bearing a taper, with verses pinned on her back (S.D. after II. iv. 16). Ironically, Shakespeare inserts the episode in which Gloucester

135

unmasks Simpcox (II. i. 57–160) between the scene in which the audience sees Eleanor taken conjuring (I. iv) and the announcement of her crime to the king and court (II. i. 161–201). The good duke can see through the false miracle of St Albans' shrine, but has not been able to penetrate his wife's deceptions, though scene juxtaposition suggests an equivalence between the two. When Gloucester is consequently removed from power, Henry becomes even more vulnerable. Indirectly, the ambition of an aspiring and ungovernable woman seems a chief cause of the crumbling of the crowned king's rule.

Interestingly, Foxe's account of Eleanor's acts is more ambivalent than Shakespeare's. Foxe waffles about the degree to which Eleanor was actually guilty of a crime, suggesting that perhaps she was simply set up by the Bishop of Winchester because she "seemed then to favour and savour of that religion set forth by Wickliff" (Foxe 1877: 707).[2] Not only was she the victim of Winchester's hatred of her husband, but also of his hatred for her religious views. Shakespeare makes it clear that Winchester craftily entraps Eleanor to discredit her husband, but he does not bring out her supposed proto-Protestantism, nor does he exculpate her of the crime of demonic conjuration. In fact, we see her conjuration enacted on stage. There is in this case little doubt that the overreaching woman bears the immediate blame for her husband's fall and, consequently, some of the blame for Henry's.

The opening two acts of this play are freighted with vignettes of treason and dangerous theatricality as the anxiety about the king who is no king gets displaced on to a woman and the needy, not-too-clever Simpcox. Both are subject to punishments that expose who they "really" are. The whip reveals that Simpcox is no invalid, and the ordeal of the sheet and taper literally exposes Eleanor's body as that of a criminal. The combat between Horner and his apprentice seems calculated to produce the same effect of power's exposure of truth. In an epistemological frame that assumes real essences to be separable from deceptive appearances, juridical and other social mechanisms are necessary for making "truth" visible. In *Henry VI*, however, the cultural rituals and the people vested with the power to make distinctions between truth and falsehood are frequently compromised. The authority of the Church, as figured by the Bishop of Winchester, is compromised, for example, by

Winchester's ambition and malice. "Good" Duke Humphrey, who spies much chicanery, can't discern his wife's. And, as we shall see, the Horner episode makes a mockery of the chivalric trial by combat through which truth was traditionally distinguished from lies.

The Horner affair involves an apprentice, Peter, accusing his master of having said that the Duke of York was the proper heir to the English throne (I. iii. 183–4). His master in turn accuses the apprentice of lying because he resented being reproved for a fault by his master (I. iii. 197–200). Who is a lying knave and who a true man? Duke Humphrey assigns man and master to the trial of single combat to determine the answer. In the event, Peter Thump the apprentice defeats his master who confesses treason and dies (II. iii. 94), but the combat is moved close to farce by the fact that the master turns up drunk and the apprentice does not know how to handle a sword. The audience beholds something perilously close to a parody of a chivalric encounter. The traditional – and highly theatrical – rituals by which truth and falsehood are distinguished no longer seem adequate to the task. Moreover, while Horner dies, York – whose armor the luckless Horner was scouring when he supposedly utters his treacherous remarks – goes on to suborn Jack Cade to play the part of Mortimer's descendant and so to lodge a counterclaim to the throne. In short, if Providential justice might be imagined as operative in the case of Horner, it seems stunningly blind to the naked and treasonous ambition of a York who throughout the Horner episodes piously insists on his own loyalty to Henry and his horror that anyone would dare treasonously to assert his claim to the throne.

York's suborning of Cade simply underscores the link between unsanctioned theatricality and treason permeating this play. On the one hand, in his advocacy of those who go in "clouted shoes", Cade's is the ventriloquized voice of the common man speaking against the privileges of the rich and the literate (Patterson 1989: 48–51). But he has been set to his rebellion by York, and part of his role is to claim to be in the line of descent from Mortimer. Consequently, he fabricates for himself a royal pedigree, arrogates to himself the right to make the laws of England, to sentence men to death, and to redistribute property. But when he is killed by the property-loving Iden, this again does nothing to stop the violence erupting in England.

York survives, now openly imagining himself a king, and claiming *both* that he has a blood claim to the throne and that he acts more like a king than does Henry. "I am far better born than is the King;/More like a king, more kingly in my thoughts;/But I must make fair weather yet a while,/Till Henry be more weak and I more strong" (V. i. 28–31). York never does become strong enough to seize and wear the crown, except the paper crown Margaret in derision puts on his head before murdering him. Margaret's actions again turn the world upside down as the sacred ritual of a king's coronation is parodied and emptied of meaning.

Only Richard III, York's son, fulfills his father's dream of wearing the crown and assuming the role of king. And with Richard the antitheatricality of the first tetralogy reaches its apogee. Richard's masterful use of theatrical skills stands in vivid contrast to Henry's utter transparency and inability to disguise a single thing about himself. A guileless, open man, Henry is vulnerable precisely because he lacks all powers of pretense, openly confessing he would rather be a shepherd than inhabit the place destiny has thrust upon him. It is the enemies of his reign who have cornered the market in theatricality which with Richard becomes the essence of his being and of his kingship (Watson 1990: 100–10). As early as *3 Henry VI*, Richard says that, born with teeth, he will "play the dog" (V. vi. 77), and in the play that bears his name he makes himself the leading actor in successive scenes of dissembling, from the pretense of being smitten with Anne (I. ii) to the pretense before the mayor and citizens of London that he eschews the crown and would rather spend his time in prayer, a role that Buckingham characterizes as "the maid's part, still answer nay, and take it" (III. vii. 51).

But while there is no doubt that Richard's histrionic skills are useful to him in winning the throne, there is also no doubt in this play that he is evil, and that England suffers from his tyranny. The treacherous Machiavel is king, and his theatricality seems the antithesis of legitimate authority as embodied in the God-fearing Richmond. Richard's characterization is of a piece with the rest of the first tetralogy which sees in the monstrous ego of the self-fashioning actor a threat to all forms of social stability and cultural legitimacy. The crowned king having, for all practical purposes, abdicated his throne, England is at the mercy of imposters and upstarts, her cultural rituals emptied of their binding and legitimating force. In the most pejorative sense, all is theater, pretense, and ambition.

In my reading of the *Henry VI* plays, then, the antitheatrical discourse generally available in the culture from the writings of Northbrooke, Gosson, Lodge, and Stubbes is ready-to-hand to provide one frame of intelligibility through which to map the descent into social chaos. Relatively insignificant imposters such as Saunder Simpcox are linked, by scene juxtaposition and the language of ambition and disguise, to overrreaching women such as Eleanor Cobham, seditious class bounders such as Cade, and finally, throne snatchers such as Richard. All the negative associations of theatricality familiar from the writings of Stubbes or Gosson are satirically mobilized: associations between theatricality and Catholicism, class insurgency, traffic with demons, sexual licentiousness, and the gender disorder associated with crossdressing. At the same time that these plays denigrate theatricality, of course, they also reveal its power. Those who lack theatrical skills, such as Henry, are vulnerable to those, such as Richard, who possess them in abundance. What the plays can't do, however, is overtly figure legitimacy in theatrical terms. Richmond may, with Stanley, plot to dissemble the extent of Stanley's involvement with Richard in order to save George Stanley's life, but that is one of his few deceptions. Richmond stands, above all, for unitary English truth. Through his essential virtue and inherent kingliness, we are to believe, England is saved from the monstrous rule of theatrical imposters and seditious upstarts.

THE HENRIAD AND THE REWRITING OF THEATRICALITY

As everyone knows, what has come to be called the second tetralogy differs markedly from the first in stagecraft and in its representations of kingship and of nation. While, for example, the earlier plays employ an episodic structure that effectively suggests the chaos of civil war, the later histories are at once less prone to allegory and emblematic episodes such as the Simpcox scenes and more rigorously shaped to give dramatic form to the materials of chronicle history. In terms of subject matter, while the histories from *Richard II* to *Henry V* were written *after* the *Henry VI* plays, they deal with historical material directly *prior* to Henry's troubled reign. Paradoxically, though they represent events preceding the Wars of the Roses, the plays of the second tetralogy bear the imprint of modernity in ways the plays of the earlier tetralogy do not. Nowhere is this more apparent than in their treatment of theatricality.

As I have discussed, in the early histories theatricality is a mark of the monstrous and the seditious. In a way that resonates comfortably with the polemic of the antitheatrical tracts, threats to social order are embodied in women who wear men's clothes (Joan of Arc) or who dress above their station (Eleanor Cobham) or in men who appropriate the lineage of the aristocracy (Cade) or who pretend, constantly, to be what they are not (Richard III). By contrast, in the second tetralogy, the dream of a natural social order purged of the distortions of theatricality is rendered anachronistic. Even Gaunt, as he dies, can speak of an Edenic England only in the past tense and only in elegiac tones. Consequently, theatricality cannot simply be hived off from the center of culture and represented as demonic or as a mere distortion of nature. Instead, in the second tetralogy the inescapability of theatricality in a world of lost essences is implicitly and with difficulty acknowledged. Rather than being opposed to kingship, theatricality is revealed as interior to it, though now rewritten as statescraft. Consequently, the overt deployment of an antitheatrical discourse, so prominent in the first tetralogy, largely disappears in the second, even as performative prowess, rather than blood lineage, becomes the *sine qua non* for kingship.

It is significant, moreover, that the second tetralogy marks its modernity partly by depicting within its fifteenth-century landscape the contemporary London world of an Eastcheap tavern, and that that tavern in its turn evokes the world of the London theater, as do the choruses of *Henry V*. A portion of the modernity of these plays lies in their knowingness about their own status as dramas enacted in a particular cultural setting, and part of the modernity of their representations of kingship stems from the implicit connection they forge between the base trade of commercial playing and the exalted arts of statescraft (Kastan 1986). Rewriting a discourse that equates the theatrical with the marginal, these plays reveal the theatricality at the center of the culture.

The interesting questions about theatricality in this second tetralogy center on Hal, though it is Richard II who is by critics most often called "the player king." But Richard's "actorliness" is different *both* from Richard III's and from Hal's. Richard is probably the monarch with the best blood claim to the throne in any of the Shakespearean history plays. Yet what the play seems to acknowledge, with appropriate ritual and nostalgia, is that the legitimacy of blood is no longer enough. Richard's actorliness is not demonic like Richard III's, not a sign of overarching ambition and pretense. Rather, his gorgeous but ineffective rhetoric and his histrionic poses reveal the emptiness of legitimate titles severed from pragmatic skills necessary to invest them with meaning. Blessed with a powerful claim to the throne, Richard wastes both time and opportunity in maintaining his right. In his depiction, theatricality comes primarily to signal hollowness, and to that extent it resonates with the antitheatricality of a Gosson berating actors for not "really" being the figures they personate.

The recognition *Richard II* thrusts upon the spectator – that neither lineage nor a histrionic temper is sufficient to secure and retain a throne – raises the question of what *can* constitute effective monarchy in conditions of modernity. Unexpectedly, in the Henry IV plays, the tavern is both the place where the pressure of modernity is most felt, and where possible solutions to this question of effective kingship are worked out. Significantly, the Boar's Head tavern seems not to be congruent, historically, with the world of early fifteenth-century England in which it is anachronistically inserted. As many commentators have noted, there is little doubt that it very much resembles taverns in late sixteenth-century London. It is here that the prince drinks the beer and sees the peach-colored stockings that would, respectively, have been consumed and worn in Shakespeare's own London.[3] It is from the tavern that one gets a sense of the urban commercial world in which the London theater had its own existence and a sense of the range of people who might have paid to see history plays, the theater's representation of England's national past. In Shakespeare's depiction, the Boar's Head tavern is both a social gathering point and a bustling economic enterprise: a place of consumption for many and of profit for some. Drink and sex – in the person of Doll Tearsheet – are on offer in the tavern, but so, too, is entertainment. Musicians are summoned to the Boar's Head in Part 2, and in both Part 1 and Part 2 storytelling, jests, and theatricals constitute a central part of tavern life. Mistress Quickly, as the entrepreneur in this scene, seems to enjoy a degree of material success. She has had enough money, for example, to lend some to Falstaff, which she is trying to reclaim at the beginning of 2 *Henry IV*, and she has plate and tapestries that could, as Falstaff urges, be pawned for more cash (2 *Henry IV* II. i. 140–52). Falstaff leeches off Quickly because the tavern provides her with an income, something to leech *from*; and 1 and 2 *Henry IV* are littered with small details indicating Quickly's modest material success. Possessed of plate and tapestries, she also, if the beadle in 2 *Henry IV* V. iv is to be believed, has a dozen cushions for the seats of the tavern, one of which has been used to pad Doll Tearsheet's stomach in order to fake a pregnancy. She has employees such as the hapless apprentice, Francis, under her control; and the wherewithal to summon a whore, Doll Tearsheet, to entertain Falstaff when he is about to depart for the war (2 *Henry IV* II. i. 163–4). In short, the tavern makes a profit by providing a sociable venue where certain commodities – food, drink, and sex – are bought and sold.

In indirect but important ways the tavern resembles the contemporary London theater. Both are commercial establishments; both are gathering places for what was commonly assumed to be the low life of the city; both are places of consumption. As Ann Cook makes clear, much besides the performance was on sale at the theater: oranges, nuts, tobacco, ale, beer, wine, broadsides (Cook 1981: 196–202). Crucially, it is in the tavern that Hal has his primary contact with the consummate role player, Falstaff, and it is in the tavern that he explicitly plays, with his friend, at being a king (1 *Henry IV* II. iv. 376–481). The most astonishing thing about their playacting sequence is that it makes kingship so self-consciously into a role to be performed. The conventions of the stage provide languages for rendering that role. Whether drawing on Lyly's Euphuistic rhetoric or the conventions of morality plays, Falstaff and Hal play at being king in terms provided by the stage. Their playlets, moreover, are performed before the admiring and critical eyes of other taverngoers, suggesting that there are informed consumers of theatrical art ready to judge the performance of any would-be king. Even Quickly, not the most sophisticated of critics, praises Falstaff for how he "holds his countenance" (1 *Henry IV* II. iv.

392) and says his performance is "as like one of these harlotry players as ever I see" (II. iv. 395–6). This is an urban culture accustomed to consuming theatrical fare, and accustomed to seeing any social role, even that of king, turned into the matter for a harlotry player to imitate.

Part of the artfulness of Shakespeare's own dramatic representations of kingship, of course, is that they pass as more true to life than what has preceded them on the stage precisely by evoking and then moving beyond either the psychomachia of the moralities or the exquisitely balanced cadences of Lyly's prose. What the scene in the tavern makes clear, however, is the theatrical pleasure the miming of greatness affords, the existence of a variety of stage languages for its enactment, and the existence of audiences accustomed to judging – with varying degrees of sophistication – such performances.

Bolingbroke nowhere shows how little he truly understands the requirements of modern kingship, its necessary embrace of theatricality in a theatrically literate culture, than when he urges his son to follow his example and keep himself from the public eye so that "By being seldom seen, I could not stir/But like a comet I was wond'red at" (*1 Henry IV* III. ii. 46–7). Bolingbroke knows the importance of self-presentation and wants to avoid the diminution of authority that supposedly followed from Richard's indiscriminate mingling with "vulgar company" (III. ii. 41), but he misjudges the necessity for the modern king constantly and publicly to perform kingship. He imagines the king as a jewel to be displayed on rare occasions, a dazzling essence, rather than a fragile construct ceaselessly recreated before the eyes of beholders. Nor can he understand that "the reformation of the prodigal prince" might be a highly effective part for a would-be king to play, a riveting first act to a much longer performance. Throughout his reign Bolingbroke must rely repeatedly on the force that brought him to the throne to maintain him there. He is, in that sense, the opposite of the merely histrionic Richard, who proved unable to command armies and to think strategically and pragmatically. But it also makes him very different from his son, who can command an army in the field, but who is also constantly alive to the benefits of staging himself advantageously before the eyes of the many publics whose allegiance he would woo, rather than coerce. Consequently, while Henry IV's hold on the throne always seems tenuous, despite his pragmatic skills, Hal's grows daily more secure.

Hal's seductive stagecraft is integral to his successful statescraft.[4] Like Cleopatra, who performs femininity with infinite, never cloying variety, Hal performs kingship with equal avidity and equal dexterity. Like Cleopatra, his objects are seduction and control. As prince, Hal early reveals his acute awareness of the importance of staging himself carefully, as when he contemplates the effect he will make when he gives over his loose ways and, reformed, begins to glitter "like bright metal on a sullen ground" (*1 Henry IV* I. ii. 212). But it is as king that he most actively puts his theatrical skills to use in the service of effective monarchy. The banishment of Falstaff performed in the public streets before a crowd of onlookers, rather than in private, is one of the first signs of his histrionic skills in action. In that episode, Hal performs kingship as an embodiment of justice. He speaks to Falstaff impersonally and formally, "I know thee not, old man, fall to thy prayers" (*2 Henry IV* V. v. 47), rather than in the teasing and colloquial terms in which exchanges between the two of them have usually been couched. And he does so before an audience which includes his old enemy, the chief justice, and his brothers. His success at comporting himself like a monarch is signaled by the smug approbation of John: "I like this fair proceeding of the King's" (*2 Henry IV* V. v. 97). Hal has behaved cruelly to his old tavern mate, but in John's eyes he has behaved like royalty, a master of statescraft.

In *Henry V* audience response repeatedly signals that Hal has mastered the art of appearing kingly. In I. i Canterbury testifies that

> The breath no sooner left his father's body,
> But that his wildness, mortified in him,
> Seem'd to die too; yea, at that very moment,
> Consideration like an angel came
> And whipt th'offending Adam out of him,
> Leaving his body as a paradise
> T'envelop and contain celestial spirits.
> Never was such a sudden scholar made;
> Never came reformation in a flood
> With such a heady currance, scouring faults;
> Nor never Hydra-headed willfulness

So soon did lose his seat (and all at once)
As in this king.

(I. i. 25–37)

As a consequence of the carefully staged scene in which Henry
takes offense at the Dauphin's gift of tennis balls, the Constable
of France warns the French king and the dauphin to take Henry
seriously: "Question your Grace the late embassadors,/With
what great state he heard their embassy,/How well supplied
with noble counsellors,/How modest in exception, and withal/
How terrible in constant resolution" (II. iv. 31–5). The list could
go on. Whether stagemanaging the scene in which Cambridge,
Grey, and Scroop in effect condemn themselves to death (II. ii)
or threatening Harfleur with the ravages of war (III. iii), Hal is
constantly aware of and in command of the impression he
is making and of how those who are audience to his performance are responding. No longer the mark of the demonic, theatricality has become a tool for effective modern kingship.

This transition is not effected without difficulty, however, and
ideological contradictions concerning theatricality are part of
what make the second tetralogy interesting. Falstaff, for
example, at the battle of Shrewsbury keeps alive the associations
of roleplaying with counterfeiting, lies, and self-serving
ambition. When he feigns death in order to avoid having to
engage in battle and then pretends to have killed the already
dead Hotspur, he opens himself to charges of dishonor as well
as deception, and he indirectly implicates Henry IV in similar
crimes. In the first half of V. iv Douglas meets Henry on the
battlefield and asks "What art thou/That counterfeit'st the
person of a King?" (1 Henry IV V. iv. 27–8). A moment later he
says, "I fear thou art another counterfeit,/And yet in faith thou
bearest thee like a king" (35–6). In the second half of the scene
Falstaff soliloquizes on the virtues of counterfeiting: "'Sblood,
'twas time to counterfeit, or that hot termagant Scot had paid
me scot and lot too. Counterfeit? I lie, I am no counterfeit. To
die is to be a counterfeit, for he is but the counterfeit of a man
who hath not the life of a man; but to counterfeit dying, when
a man thereby liveth, is to be no counterfeit, but the true and
perfect image of life indeed" (V. iv. 113–19).[5]

Falstaff's paradoxical defense of feigning is clever and pragmatic; it is also limited by his starting assumption: namely, that

to stay alive is the only important value. While the fat knight critiques the vain honor of dead men, he himself is implicitly critiqued – in the context of the battlefield, standing over the body of Hotspur – by the courage of Hotspur and his fidelity to values Falstaff does not recognize as important. A debunking voice, Falstaff is also debunked; and the pointed analogy between his dishonourable counterfeiting and Henry's, who has many men marching in his coats, also undermines the king (Winny 1968: 120). To multiply simulacra of oneself merely to stay alive – which is what the analogy to Falstaff's behavior seems to imply – is not a performance of kingship an audience can applaud. At once cowardly and deceptive, it also starkly reveals what must be concealed: that "the king" is a role that can be assumed. It is all a matter of "coats" and inhabiting them convincingly.

Hal does not make his father's mistakes. *His* role at Shrewsbury is an heroic one; more importantly, he makes himself seem – not replicable – but unique, irreplaceable. Hotspur has been England's chivalric lodestar. As his wife says: "By his light/Did all the chevalry of England move/To do brave acts" (2 *Henry IV* II. iii. 19–21). Hal knows there must not appear to be two such lights in England or the desired impression of his unique princeliness is made vulnerable. Consequently, at Shrewsbury he challenges Hotspur for the right to play, solo and uncontested, the role of Prince of Wales.

> I am the Prince of Wales, and think not, Percy,
> To share with me in glory any more.
> Two stars keep not their motion in one sphere,
> Nor can one England brook a double reign
> Of Harry Percy and the Prince of Wales.
>
> (1 *Henry IV* V. iv. 63–7)

His subsequent defeat of Hotspur, orchestrated as the emotional climax of the play, does much to win the theater audience's assent to Hal's unique right to his title, even though that audience knows full well that the prince has carefully stagemanaged just this response. Hal is playing a part, calculating effects, but doing so with a brio that seems unique. Kingship may be only a part, but Hal's performance of it makes the possibility of other equally skilled performances seem unimaginable.

In 2 *Henry IV* it is the title of king, not of prince, that Hal claims at play's end, and in *Henry V* his successful performance of kingship depends largely on his shrouding of personal opportunism in a language of the national good. It is not his survival, but England's, that is made to seem constantly on the line. Yet even in the midst of Hal's triumphant display of theatrical powers, a dis-ease about monarchical theatricality can still surface. It is heard, for example, when the skeptical Williams gives a tart reply to the disguised Henry's claim that "I myself heard the King say he would not be ransom'd" (*Henry V* IV. i. 190–1). To which Williams replies: "Ay, he said so, to make us fight cheerfully; but when our throats are cut, he may be ransom'd, and we ne'er the wiser" (IV. i. 192–4). Williams is well aware that the king has the potential to act a part merely to elicit a particular response from his audience and aware that the king may not "mean" what he says. His reply seems particularly fitting in that the audience knows that at that moment it is Henry himself who, in disguise, is attempting by his praise of "the king" to elicit a committed and patriotic response from Williams. "Sincerity" does not cease to be an issue in a world in which theatricality pervades every aspect of existence, but in *Henry V* it is a worry pushed to the margins of a text that in the main is celebratory of the skills of the histrionically resourceful Henry. There is no Gaultree, for example, in *Henry V*. Hal never simply gives his word and then reneges, as does his brother John. His duplicity, when there is any, is veiled, spiking the guns of those who would read his histrionics through an antitheatrical rhetoric of lies, deception, and counterfeiting. It is Falstaff, and John, who bear the stigma of such rhetoric.

One can see Shakespeare's careful construction of a king who "acts," but does not necessarily thereby "lie," by looking at one of Henry's most striking scenes, his wooing of Katherine of France. Nowhere, perhaps, is the modernity of the world of the play indicated more sharply than in its handling of Henry's prospective marriage. Wives, obviously, are essential to most of Shakespeare's kings in that they are the vehicles through whom heirs are produced and lineages extended. In the first tetralogy, as we saw, wives were a source of great anxiety. The strong-willed, theatrical women of the early histories are demonized in part because of their supposed sexual errancy and appetites. In the second tetralogy something quite different happens. Richard II has a wife, but she is not threatening; in fact, she is little better than a shadow figure mourning the downfall of her husband, and together she and Richard do not produce an heir, another mark of ineffectiveness. The Lancastrians, father and son, mostly seem able to do without women. Henry IV has had a wife, we know, because he has a son; but she does not figure in these plays. Ever efficient, Henry has managed to make use of the reproductive labor of a woman without having her encroach in any noticeable way on his life. Anxiety about wives surfaces in the Henry IV plays in the context of Mortimer's relationship with Owen Glendower's daughter and Hotspur's relationship with his Kate. Interestingly, the anxiety here is not so much about female promiscuity as about masculine self-control. Mortimer so dotes upon his wife that he would learn her tongue and forsake his duty on the battlefield. He is, in essence, effeminated by an inability to control his passion for his wife. Hotspur, by contrast, is so comically determined *not* to be in thrall to his affection for his wife that he is frequently gracelessly abrupt in his dealings with her. When battle summons, he tells her: "This is no world/To play with mammets and to tilt with lips./We must have bloody noses and crack'd crowns,/And pass them current too" (1 *Henry IV* II. iii. 91–4). There is little doubt that there is affection in this relationship, but it expresses itself in odd and awkward ways. Neither man – both of whom would be king – performs the part of husband with grace or, in Mortimer's case, with perfect self-control. Henry IV does not perform the role at all.

Hal is as much established as an effective modern king by the representation of his courtship as by any other of his actions. After the deposition of Richard it seems that lineage alone cannot secure the right to a throne. The king acquires legitimacy by performing his role convincingly as much as by inheriting a title. This requirement extends to the king's performance of his role as husband. In this play no identity pre-exists its performative enactment. As Henry must prove himself a monarch by performance, so must he prove himself a suitor and husband. Importantly, if Hal successively assumed the titles of prince and king at the end of the earlier two plays, at the end of *Henry V* it is the title of husband which he seems bent on acquiring. It is a mark of the play's modernity that this role, like the others, must be performed to be achieved. It is also a mark of modernity that this marriage must be something more than a dynastic union in the feudal manner, must aspire, as well, to be an affective union.

A striking thing about the wooing scene is how long it is (nearly two hundred lines) and how climactically placed. Everything about the scene seems designed to transform the stark realities of a dynastic marriage into something else. In reality Katherine is a prize of war; in reality she has no choice as to whether or not to marry Henry; in reality affection probably does not matter. But a great deal of the last act is devoted to disguising or supplementing these facts. The contrast with the proposed marriage of Richmond and Elizabeth at the end of *Richard III* is instructive. By that union of "the White Rose and the Red" (*Richard III* V. v. 19) the wounds of war are to be healed and a dynasty established, just as in *Henry V*. But Elizabeth never appears on stage; no courtship scene is depicted; no emotional ties between the prospective bride and groom need to be established. Because these two bear in their blood the lineage of York and Lancaster, their marriage is assumed "true," and by it England is redeemed from illegitimate rule.

By contrast, Shakespeare contrives for Henry V an elaborate scene of courtship through which, by performance, these two actors *create* the truth of their union, one in which the stark realities of patriarchal domination are veiled by the gestures of mutuality. I have always found this scene an utterly charming and utterly disturbing performance: one which shows Hal "correcting" the faults of a Mortimer or a Hotspur, seeming to grant Katherine a degree of control she in reality lacks, and gesturing towards a mutuality belied repeatedly, but subtly, by Henry's masterful stagemanaging of the entire encounter. The length of the scene is important to its effectiveness in that it pays Katherine the compliment of having Henry seem to work hard for what he has in reality already won. The episode may have only one possible conclusion, but it takes a long time to get there. Second, the fact that the scene involves two languages seems to suggest a mutual desire for each participant to speak the other's tongue, acknowledge the other's autonomy. In reality, of course, most of the scene unrolls in English, and Henry has most of the lines, all of the long speeches. Perhaps most cleverly, the persona Henry adopts in the scene, that of "plain soldier" (V. ii. 149), makes it possible for him to seem a bit out of his depth, somewhat mitigating the harshness of the actual power relations that exist between the conquered female princess and the conquering king. For instance, when Katherine doesn't understand one of his speeches, he says:

> I will tell thee in French, which I am sure will hang upon my tongue like a new-married wife about her husband's neck, hardly to be shook off. *Je quand sur le possession de France, et quand vous avez le possession de moi* – let me see, what then? Saint Denis be my speed! – *donc votre est France and vous êtes mienne.* It is as easy for me, Kate, to conquer the kingdom as to speak so much more French. I shall never move thee in French, unless it be to laugh at me.
>
> (V. ii. 178–87)

In actuality, the real power lines between the two of them are deeply encoded in every aspect of the speech. It begins and ends in English. The first simile equates the French language hanging upon Henry's English tongue with a doting wife hanging upon her husband's neck and only with difficulty to be shaken off. The image indicates both the wife's dependent position and that of the French tongue. Moreover, Henry's French sentence begins and ends with an account of his conquests: of Katherine and of France. He enfolds her conquest of him, and so of France, safely inside his own agency. However, in other respects, the speech seems all modesty and deference, with Henry playing to the hilt the part of the linguistic incompetent. In short, to the extent that Katherine is Henry's primary audience in this scene, he does much to seem to put himself at her mercy and to create for her the illusion of choice. But to the extent that the theater audience is his target, the scene leaves no doubt that Henry is actually very much in charge, though performing with grace and tact. When Kate denies him a kiss, he replies:

> O Kate, nice customs curt'sy to great kings. Dear Kate, you and I cannot be confin'd within the weak list of a country's fashion. We are the makers of manners, Kate; and the liberty that follows our places stops the mouth of all find-faults, as I will do yours, for upholding the nice fashion of your country in denying me a kiss; therefore patiently and yielding. [Kissing her].
>
> (V. ii. 268–75)

There is little question here of a man effeminately doting on a woman's every desire; nor any question of tactlessness. This is a flawless performance of masculine control disguising itself as mutuality. It has become one of the familiar performances of modernity, and by it Henry succeeds to the title of husband, perfecting and culminating his kingship.

I agree with those critics such as James Calderwood (1979) who have seen the second tetralogy as an exploration of the performative dimensions of cultural power. The first tetralogy demonizes theatricality as the antithesis of legitimacy. The second refuses such an opposition by showing the acquisition of legitimacy through, among other things, performative skills. The difference between the two groups of plays invites comment. It is worth emphasizing that this difference is implicitly present within antitheatrical polemic itself. The chief irony of the antitheatrical tracts is that even as they castigate theatricality they reveal its inescapability. Enjoining subjects to lay aside one set of theatrical trappings (cosmetics, silks, feathers), they urge them to take up another set (woolen garments, modest ruffs, downcast eyes). Arguing for God-given identities, the tracts unwittingly reveal identities as man-made and constructed. While the first tetralogy, then, adumbrates the overt logic of the antitheatrical tracts, the second tetralogy brings to the surface their covert logic. The shift in part registers the growing self-confidence of theatrical craftsmen such as Shakespeare. Turning away from a cultural discourse that used theatricality primarily as a figure for the demonic, the illusory, and the distorted, he now writes theatricality into the central institutions of early modern culture, rather than having theatricality haunt the demonized margins of that culture.

Certainly the shift marks the modernity of the second tetralogy. The past abuts more insistently on the present in the latter set of plays than in the former. Contemporary London enters the fictive world in the form of the Boar's Head tavern, in references to "the wooden O" (*Henry V* I. i. 13) where these plays were actually being performed, and in the nod toward new ideologies of gender in the representation of Henry's marriage. The theater, like the tavern, is part of the commercial landscape of this modern London, writing and rewriting the terms in which its inhabitants understood themselves.

151

In writing the king as performer in the second tetralogy, Shakespeare certainly demystified monarchy's sacred aura (Kastan 1986). Moreover, these plays contribute to a general undermining of essentialist ideologies of social being and social place. In them the theater writes back against the overt intentions of antitheatricalists, insisting on the culturally constructed, performatively sustained dimensions of social identity. That said, not even Shakespeare's second tetralogy contests the primacy of the king's role in early modern culture. The role of king may be just that – a role to be continually secured by a forceful performance of it – but these plays do little to question that role's centrality or to imagine an England that does not define itself largely in relation to the monarchical presence. In fact, as Walter Cohen has argued, Shakespeare's histories as a group perform part of their work of cultural modernization by depicting as desirable the centralizing of political power in the hands of a single powerful monarch, and so downplaying the power of the feudal lords (Cohen 1985: 218–84). In that regard they further an absolutist agenda, but they do so by rewriting the terms in which kingship is conceived. They thus display the cultural power theater has acquired in a commercializing culture.

Many material factors had to be in place for the theater to acquire its particular importance in early modern England. The growth of London into a city able to sustain an entertainment industry, the accumulation of capital that allowed buildings to be erected solely for the staging of plays – these were necessary preconditions for the emergence of an active commercial theater. Having been established, this commercial stage *did* accrue considerable cultural power despite the language of denigration often used to discuss it. As I have attempted to show, this theater – both through its institutional practices and its fictions – was thoroughly involved in the social struggles and transformations of early modern England. Whether inviting urban wives to become theatrical spectators, rewriting the terms of monarchical legitimacy, or instantiating the female crossdresser in the cultural imaginary, the public theater was an active participant in Tudor and Stuart culture. Not simply an instrument of the monarch or the state, the stage could rewrite or destabilize the cultural narratives of socially dominant groups, though often it did neither. Wrong about many things, the antitheatricalists were thus right about the potential power of the upstart institution in their midst, though no contemporary was fully able to comprehend the complicated and often contradictory political consequences of this stage's operations. Considered across the full range of its practices, the public theater of early modern England was far from ideologically self-consistent. Therein lies its fascination and its significance for those seeking to understand the complicated conditions of constraint and possibility within which social struggle occurs.

NOTES

1 RENAISSANCE THEATER AND THE REPRESENTATION OF THEATRICAL PRACTICE

1 I am indebted throughout this work to Jonas Barish's important study, *The Antitheatrical Prejudice*, though Barish is interested in the history of ideas and I in the historically specific social struggles enacted through particular discourses.

2 For a good example of a discussion of a Shakespeare play in terms of the tension between its class and gender politics see Peter Erickson's "The Order of the Garter, the Cult of Elizabeth, and Class–Gender Tension in *The Merry Wives of Windsor*" (1987).

3 For a general overview of the ambitions of such a criticism see the introduction to *Shakespeare Reproduced: The Text in History and Ideology*, ed. Jean E. Howard and Marion F. O'Connor (1987), and for an overview of its accomplishments in regard to Shakespeare studies see that volume's lead eassy, "Political Criticism of Shakespeare," by Walter Cohen.

4 In a series of brilliant essays Louis Montrose has examined the way in which Elizabeth I used the conventions of pastoral and the resources of religious and mythological discourse to regulate the power relations of her court by creating highly artificial – and highly conventionalized – roles for herself and her courtiers to play. It is Montrose's contention that these fictions not only allowed Elizabeth to exercise power over her subjects, but also allowed her subjects to *appropriate* these fictions to gain a certain degree of power over their monarch. My point is that these activities are a striking instance of a culturally sanctioned – indeed, monarchically sanctioned – role playing. See especially his " 'Eliza, Queene of shepheardes,' and the Pastoral of Power" (1980a) and "The Elizabethan Subject and the Spenserian Text" (1986).

5 For a critique of the idea of literature as an essential, rather than an historical, category of writing see Tony Bennett (1979 and 1990: esp. 177–90).

6 Two other provocative discussions of the theater's potential destabili-

zation of dominant ideology are given by David Kastan (1986) and Steven Mullaney (1988a: esp. 1–59).

7 For a general discussion of censorship in the period see Annabel Patterson (1984). Philip Finkelpearl (1986), while not denying the existence and power of a censorship apparatus, nonetheless stresses the inefficiencies and variability of its operations in regard to the censorship of stage plays in the Jacobean period.

8 Edward Pechter (1987) is one of those who has launched an attack on political criticism of Renaissance drama. His essay, it should be noted, received the special status of publication in *PMLA*, despite the fact that it presents a relatively confused account of new historicism and its politics.

9 Tony Bennett (1987) makes a sophisticated and powerful argument that political criticism must justify itself in terms of its effectivity as intervention in changing historical circumstances. For my own extended discussion of situated knowledge production see my essay "Towards a Postmodern, Politically Committed Historical Practice" (1991b: eps. 112–21).

2 "SATHANS SYNAGOGUE"

1 The emphasis in popular literary forms catering to an emergent "middle class" on thrift, hard work, and self-discipline is discussed at length by Louis B. Wright (1935: esp. 170–200, "Lessons in Diligence and Thrift," and 228–296, "Guides to Holiness").

2 By contrast, Raphael Hythloday in Book One of Thomas More's *Utopia* (1516) attacks those who punish theft by hanging and with enormous sympathy describes the plight of those displaced by enclosures. "They leave the only homes familiar to them, and they can find no place to go. Since they cannot afford to wait for a buyer, they sell for a pittance all their household goods, which would not bring much in any case. When that little money is gone (and it's soon spent in wandering from place to place), what remains for them but to steal, and so be hanged – justly you'd say! – or to wander and beg? And yet if they go tramping, they are jailed as sturdy beggars. They would be glad to work, but they can find no one who will hire them. There is no need for farm labor, in which they have been trained, when there is no land left to be plowed. One herdsman or shepherd can look after a flock of beasts large enough to stock an area that would require many hands if it were plowed and reaped" (pp. 14–15).

3 For a good brief discussion of the way in which the aristocracy in England converted to commercial activities before the aristocracy in other European countries, see Perry Anderson (1974: esp. 125–42).

4 William Perkins in his *A Treatise of the Vocations, or Callings of Men*, originally published in 1603, insists that men are called to their places and their vocations in the social order by God and that social distinctions and differences are appointed by God: "persons are distinguished by order, whereby God hath appointed, that in every

societie one person should be above or under another; not making all equall, as though the bodie should be all head and nothing else: but even in degree and order, he hath set a distinction, that one should be above another" (Perkins, 1612: 755). He viciously attacks vagrants and masterless men as drones; and he, too, attacks excess in dress: "the meaner sort now adaies spend that they get in fine apparell, and good cheare: and by this meanes the house of God is lesse regarded; for every common man now adaies must bee a gentleman, and it is very hard sometimes for a stranger to discerne the master from the servant: and there is such excesse in all degrees, that now for daily attire, the noblest are the plainest" (754).

5 Franco Moretti, Louis Montrose, and Jean-Christophe Agnew also discuss the new uses, and new prevalence, of the idea in English Renaissance culture of man as actor. Each examines aspects of social and economic change accompanying this ideological shift. See Moretti 1982: 7–40; Montrose 1980b: 51–74; and Agnew 1986.

6 For examinations of the masculine anxiety generated by Elizabeth see Montrose (1983: 61–94) and Erickson (1987: 116–40). For a discussion of the polemical literature concerning women's place see Woodbridge (1984), and for a broad consideration of gender tension in the period see Newman (1991), Underdown (1987), and Amussen (1988). Unlike some critics I do not see gender struggles in the Renaissance simply as a displacement of other forms of social conflict, though women *did* sometimes function as scapegoats and objects of displaced anxiety and fear. Rather I believe the terms of the gender system itself were under contest, creating a distinguishable, though not autonomous, axis of social struggle.

7 Ringler (1942: 26–8) argues that the City probably paid for Gosson's first tract and Anthony Munday's *A Second and Third Blast of Retrait from Plaies and Theaters,* and also undoubtedly blocked the public printing of Thomas Lodge's *A Reply to Gosson's Schoole of Abuse.* Kinney (1974: 17, note 40), however, argues that Gosson probably was not supported by the City since his fortunes did not at once improve and because there is no clear link between his case and that of Anthony Munday. To me the evidence in Gosson's case is inconclusive.

8 See Bergeron (1971 and 1985) for a general discussion of the nature of civil pageantry in this period and of the iconography used to honor Elizabeth and James. See Yates (1975: 29–87) for detailed consideration of representations of Elizabeth as Astraea, and Goldberg (1983: 29–33) for an examination of the differing ways in which Elizabeth and James used and participated in pageants, progresses, and masques.

9 For a good discussion of the representation of the City in the pageantry of the Stuart Lord Mayor's show, see Paster (1985: 48–64).

10 I am indebted to Theodore Leinwand's presentations on the middling sort at the Modern Language Association convention in 1991 and the Shakespeare Association of America convention in 1992.

3 ANTITHEATRICALITY STAGED

1 I discuss the relationship of text to context more fully in "The New Historicism in Renaissance Studies" (1986).

2 For an excellent discussion of the commercial imperatives governing theatrical production and the theater's distance both from social practices and from prescriptive literature see McLuskie (1989: esp. 224–9).

3 Julia Gasper (1990: esp. 74) argues that Dekker's brand of militant Protestantism was more internationalist than purely nationalist, since he advocated an alliance of Protestant powers against the Catholic anti-Christ. That Dekker did argue for an alliance, in particular of England with the Netherlands, does not in my view erase the strongly patriotic cast of this play and its designation of the English monarch as the pre-eminent champion of the Protestant cause.

4 Gasper (1990: 80–96) argues that while Dekker idealized Elizabeth he also wished to critique her for insufficient zeal in the Protestant cause and especially for the execution of Essex, the Protestant champion. This does not fully explain why her realm is described as a sink of iniquities in ways that make it seem perilously similar to the Whore of Babylon's dominions.

5 Rossiter (1961: 67) is typical of most of the play's thematic critics when he says: "Deception by appearances in love is patently what most of *Much Ado* is 'about'." Other critics take a metadramatic tack. Huston (1981: 2), for example, sees many of Shakespeare's early comedies dramatizing and celebrating the artist's playful ordering of the world through dramatic art. In *Much Ado*, however, Huston argues: "Shakespeare may be dramatizing reservations he is beginning to feel about his art and about the relationship between it and reality. He may be dramatically confronting the problem of recognizing that there are limits to his assimilative powers, that reality may sometimes successfully resist his attempts to play with it, even in art" (142).

6 I am indebted throughout the ensuing discussion to Michel Foucault's investigations (1980) of the interconnections between power and knowledge.

7 All quotations from Shakespeare's plays are taken from *The Riverside Shakespeare* (Evans 1974).

8 For an important discussion of the discursive production of desire and of gendered subjectivities, see Henriques (1984: esp. 203–63).

9 Cook (1986: 192) argues that Hero's silence elicits male fears that women are not readable and calls forth their repeated rewritings of her. For a view of Beatrice quite different from my own, see the rest of Cook's article in which she presents Beatrice as inscribed within a male subject position and so posing no threat to the masculine social order.

157

4 THE MATERIALITY OF IDEOLOGY

1 S. P. Zitner (1958: 206–8) explores the extent to which Gosson's account of the Elizabethan playgoing audience in the body of *The Schoole of Abuse* draws upon passages in Ovid's *Art of Love*. He concludes that Gosson's descriptions should not be taken as an unmediated eyewitness report of Elizabethan theatergoing. Gosson's debt to Ovid, as well as his polemic intentions, must be taken into account before one accepts his treatise as description of objective fact. In this essay, however, I am more interested in the concluding epistle to the gentlewomen of London than in the body of the tract. More importantly, however, I assume that all of Gosson's tract is ideological and interested, rather than dispassionately objective. I am concerned with why Gosson and his fellow antitheatricalists circulated certain narratives (whatever their source) about women at the theater; and I wish to offer a counter-account of what the middle-class woman's presence in that cultural space may have signified in terms of changing social relations in early modern England.

2 On 1 November 1987 Hedda Nussbaum called the police who came and removed 6-year-old Lisa and 16-month-old Mitchell Steinberg from the apartment Nussbaum shared with Steinberg. Both Lisa and Nussbaum had been severely beaten, and Lisa died four days later. In treating Nussbaum for her many injuries, doctors had to insert silicon tubes to allow one of her eyes to drain properly. Her exact words of explanation were that Steinberg had "a fear of being stared at and repeatedly poked her in the eyes for this offense" (*New York Times*, 1 December 1988).

3 I owe a special debt to the work of Walter Cohen (1985) for insisting that one pay attention to the theatrical mode of production and the material conditions of playgoing when considering the theater's role in social transformation.

4 For a useful summary of critiques and extensions of Althusser's work see T. Boswell *et al.* (1986: 5–22).

5 For the idea of disidentification see M. Pecheux (1982: 158–63). For a discussion of the multiple positioning of subjects in complex societies, and of the multiple axes of social struggle, see C. Mouffe, (1988: 31–45).

6 This critique has by now become a commonplace. It is an indication of changes within new historicism itself that in *Shakespearean Negotiations: The Circulation of Social Energy in Renaissance England*, Stephen Greenblatt writes that "the circulation of social energy by and through the stage was not part of a single coherent, totalizing system. Rather, it was partial, fragmentary, conflictual; elements were crossed, torn apart, recombined, set against each other; particular social practices were magnified by the stage, others diminished, exalted, evacuated" (Greenblatt 1988: 19).

7 A number of scholars have dealt with this issue. For an overview

of the debates see my essay "Crossdressing, the Theater and Gender Struggle in Early Modern England" (1988a: 418–40) and the revision of that essay in the next chapter of this book.

8 The standard work on this topic is Alice Clark's (1919) *Working Life of Women in the Seventeenth Century*. An updated version of Clark's position is Susan Cahn's (1987) *Industry of Devotion: The Transformation of Women's Work in England 1500–1660*.

5 POWER AND EROS

1 I am grateful to many people, especially Phyllis Rackin and Joseph Cleary, for giving me excellent critiques of my essay, "Crossdressing, the Theatre, and Gender Struggle in Early Modern England" (Howard 1988a), from which this chapter is derived. My argument here about the kinds of gender struggle enacted through crossdressing practices and representations remains virtually unchanged from that posited in the earlier essay. What *has* changed is my recognition that I need to separate more clearly issues concerning gender, that is, what a culture defines as masculine and feminine difference, from issues concerning sexuality, that is, object choice and modalities of erotic desire. I have been pushed to see the necessity of doing this by the excellent work of Valerie Traub in particular (see Traub 1992: 91–116). I received Jonathan Goldberg's *Sodometries* too late in the publication process of this book to do more than acknowledge here how incisive I find his commentary on criticism of the early modern transvestite stage, even when I disagree with some of his conclusions (Goldberg 1992: 105–43).

In this chapter I no longer speak of a sex-gender system as a single phenomenon. Gayle Rubin brought that concept to prominence in her pathbreaking essay "The Traffic in Women" (1975). Nine years later in "Thinking Sex" (1984) Rubin wrote that "although sex and gender are related, they are not the same thing, and they form the basis of two distinct arenas of social practice. In contrast to my perspective in 'The Traffic in Women,' I am now arguing that it is essential to separate gender and sexuality analytically to more accurately reflect their separate social existence" (308). In this chapter, while my focus remains primarily on struggles over gender definitions and hierarchies, I also attempt more carefully to separate gender from sexuality and to look at the ways crossdressing practices and representations may have had bearing on the channeling of erotic energy in early modern England, as well as on the structuring of gender relations.

2 Prior criticism on transvestite actors and on dramatic representations of crossdressing is extensive and good. In regard to boy actors who played women's roles, Laura Levine (1986) argues that this practice brought to the surface deep-seated fears that the self was not stable and fixed but unstable and monstrous and infinitely malleable unless strictly controlled. Behind the repeated protestations that the boy actors will be made effeminate by wearing

women's clothing, she argues, lies the fear they will be found to have no essential being. By contrast, Stephen Greenblatt argues that an all-male acting troupe was the natural and unremarkable product of a culture whose conception of gender was "teleologically male" (1988: 88). Lisa Jardine (1983: 9–36) sees the Renaissance public theater as in large measure designed for the gratification of male spectators and argues that in many cases it was homoerotic passion that the boy actors aroused in their male audience. Kathleen McLuskie (1987) in effect critiques this position by arguing that it collapses theatrical practice with real life and that in performance the sex of the actor is irrelevant and, on the Renaissance stage, conventional. A similar divergence of opinion characterizes scholarship on the presence of crossdressing in dramatic works of the period. Juliet Dusinberre, for example, argues that plays of crossdressing were sites where the freedom of women to play with gender identity was explored (1975: 231–71), while Clara Claiborne Park suggests that women who crossdress in these scripts doff their disguises willingly, providing the – to men – gratifying spectacle of spunky women who voluntarily tame themselves to suit male expectations (Park 1980: 100–16). Phyllis Rackin and Catherine Belsey both argue that at least in some instances crossdressing on the stage opens up the possibility of revealing the fluidity and artificiality of gender, thus toppling the essentialist binarism used to hold women in an inferior place (Rackin 1987 and Belsey 1985b).

3 I am extremely grateful to Professor Benbow for sharing his research with me. The following material is taken from his transcription of records from the Repertories of the Aldermen's Court in the London City Record Office and from the Bridewell Court Minute Books between approximately 1565 and 1605.

4 Professor Michael Shapiro kindly called my attention to the fact that in recounting Johanna Goodman's case I originally failed to note that her husband was also punished for this attempt to pass her off as his male servant.

5 P. Parker (1993) gives a very useful account of the divisions *within* medical discourse concerning the Galenic one-sex model, as well as reminding us that medical discourse was just *one* of many languages of sexual difference and definition in the period.

6 As Norbert Elias and others have noted, in such passages we witness the highly mediated repercussions of the transition from a feudal culture, in which military prowess was required of the ruling orders, to a courtier culture, in which the arts of civility and social negotiation are more urgent (1939).

7 For a venomous attack on the theatricality of the Catholic Mass and the sexual excesses and crimes encouraged by the wearing of ornate vestments by lewd priests, see Thomas Bacon (1637: esp. 72–5).

8 For discussion of these disciplining rituals, see Martin Ingram (1985b: 166–97); David Underdown (1985: 116–36); and Natalie Davis (1978: 147–90).

9 I think it is impossible to give a single answer to Joan Kelly's

famous question "Did Women have a Renaissance?" (1984: 19–50). If Juliet Dusinberre's account (1975) of the freedoms opening up for middle-class women in the Renaissance seems to take too little account of the recuperative powers of patriarchal systems, Lawrence Stone's more sober account (1977) of the intensification of patriarchy toward the end of the sixteenth century, especially among the upper classes, tends simply to assign to patriarchy the absolute power it claimed for itself and to ignore the possibilities for women's resistance, which it has been the work of feminist scholars such as Catherine Belsey (1985a: esp. 129–221) and others to explore. We know that the gender system *changed* in the Renaissance as new family structures emerged, as patterns of work and production changed, etc.; but change does not necessarily mean progress or the amelioration of oppression, at least not for all groups of women. Feminist scholarship is in the process of discovering where these changes enabled instances of resistance and female empowerment, as well as the many ways in which change simply meant the old oppression in new guises.

10 For useful anthologies of writings by early modern women see Betty Travitsky (1981) and Katharina M. Wilson (1987). Suzanne W. Hull (1982) usefully documents the books printed for a putatively female readership during this period. In addition there are also now several collections of critical essays dealing primarily or exclusively with Renaissance texts authored by women. See Margaret P. Hannay (1985); Marybeth Rose (1986); and Anne M. Haselkorn and Betty Travitsky (1990). Book-length studies of early modern women writers are also beginning to appear. See, for example, Mary Ellen Lamb (1990) and Ann Rosalind Jones (1990).

11 For important studies of the juxtaposition of patriarchal absolutism and contractual theories of state and family relations, see Gordon Schochet (1975) and Carole Pateman (1988). For a fascinating examination of how Restoration drama embodies these changing ideologies of marriage and authority, see Susan Staves (1979).

12 For the view that in early modern England homoeroticism was less threatening, to men, than male–female sexuality, see Stephen Orgel's important essay, "Nobody's Perfect" (1989).

13 For a fuller exploration of the relationship between class and sexuality as represented on the early modern stage see my essay "Sex and Social Conflict: The Erotics of *The Roaring Girl*" (Howard 1992: 170–90).

14 For a much less political reading of the play see my own account of the orchestration of *Twelfth Night* (Howard 1984). In that piece, while accurately mapping the actual and metaphorical disguises in the play, I did not explore the political implications of the text's insistence on the return to an "undisguised" state – what that meant for aspiring servants, independent women, etc. In short, I accepted the play's dominant ideologies as a mimesis of the true and natural order of things.

15 Here I am agreeing with Karen Newman's view (1987) that Portia

is an unruly woman who challenges masculine rhetorical hegemony and intervenes in the traffic in women upon which Renaissance patriarchal authority depended.

16 For good discussion of the disruptive effect of the epilogue, see Belsey (1985b: 166–90) and Rackin (1987: 29–41).

17 All quotations are from Andor Gomme's New Mermaid edition of *The Roaring Girl* (1976).

18 For a good discussion of both Moll Frith and Long Meg of Westminster, see Simon Shepherd (1981: esp. 67–92).

19 Jonathan Dollimore (1987: 53–81) argues that female crossdressing can, in some circumstances, be a mode of transgression and not an exemplification of false consciousness. I found particularly useful his critique of the essentialist theories of subjectivity underlying the assumption, in many discussions of female crossdressing, that it is a social practice that distorts or erases authentic female identity.

6 KINGS AND PRETENDERS

1 For an important discussion of the possible relationship between Joan's representation and anxiety about Queen Elizabeth's power see L. Marcus (1988: 66–105). For further discussion of Joan's ideological role see G. Jackson (1988).

2 Foxe speculates that if Eleanor had really been guilty she would not have been punished only with public shaming and banishment. For the stage, of course, such spectacles of shame are dramatically riveting. See, for example, the shaming of Jane Shore in Heywood's *Edward IV*.

3 For a good discussion of anachronism in the history plays see Rackin (1990: 86–145).

4 For an extensive discussion of Hal as a metadramatic representation of the playwright see J. Calderwood (1979: esp. 162–81).

5 C. L. Barber (1959: 205–13) argues that Falstaff serves as a ritual scapegoat figure in these plays, bearing off the "bad luck" of his father's and of Richard's reigns. In my reading, it is primarily the onus of deceptive theatricality that Falstaff must exorcise.

BIBLIOGRAPHY

Agnew, J.-C. (1986) *Worlds Apart: The Market and the Theatre in Anglo-American Thought, 1550–1750,* Cambridge: Cambridge University Press.

Althusser, L. (1971) "Ideology and Ideological State Apparatuses (Notes Towards an Investigation)," in *Lenin and Philosophy and Other Essays,* New York: Monthly Review Press: 127–86.

Amussen, S. (1988) *An Ordered Society: Gender and Class in Early Modern England,* Oxford: Basil Blackwell.

Anderson Jr, D. (1960) "Kingship in Ford's *Perkin Warbeck,*" *English Literary History* 27: 177–93.

Anderson, P. (1974) *Lineages of the Absolutist State,* London: New Left Books.

Andreadis, H. (1989) "The Sapphic-Platonics of Katherine Philips, 1632–1664," *Signs* 15: 34–60.

Austern, L. (1989) " 'Sing Againe Syren': The Female Musician and Sexual Enchantment in Elizabethan Life and Literature," *Renaissance Quarterly* XLII: 420–48.

Barber, C. (1959) *Shakespeare's Festive Comedy: A Study of Dramatic Form and its Relation to Social Custom,* Princeton: Princeton University Press.

Barish, J. (1981) *The Antitheatrical Prejudice,* Berkeley: University of California Press.

Barker, F. (1984) *The Tremulous Private Body: Essays on Subjection,* London: Methuen.

Barton, A. (1977) "He that Plays the King: Ford's *Perkin Warbeck* and the Stuart History Play," in *English Drama: Forms and Development,* ed. Marie Axton and Raymond Williams, Cambridge: Cambridge University Press: 69–93.

Becon, T. (1637) *The Displaying of the Popish Masse,* London, STC 1719.

Beier, A. (1983) *The Problem of the Poor in Tudor and Early Stuart England,* London: Methuen.

—— (1985) *Masterless Men: The Vagrancy Problem in England 1560–1640,* London: Methuen.

Belsey, C. (1980) *Critical Practice,* London: Methuen.

163

____ (1985a) *The Subject of Tragedy: Identity and Difference in Renaissance Drama*, New York: Methuen.

____ (1985b) "Disrupting Sexual Difference: Meaning and Gender in the Comedies," in *Alternative Shakespeares*, ed. John Drakakis, London: Methuen: 166–90.

Bennett, T. (1979) *Formalism and Marxism*, London: Methuen.

____ (1987) "Texts in History: The Determinations of Readings and Their Texts," in *Post-Structuralism and the Question of History*, ed. D. Attridge *et al.*, Cambridge: Cambridge University Press.

____ (1990) *Outside Literature*, London: Routledge.

Berger Jr, H. (1981) "Marriage and Mercifixion in *The Merchant of Venice*: The Casket Scene Revisited," *Shakespeare Quarterly* 32: 155–62.

____ (1982) "Against the Sink-a-Pace: Sexual and Family Politics in *Much Ado About Nothing*," *Shakespeare Quarterly* 33: 302–13.

Bergeron, D. (1971) *English Civic Pageantry 1558–1642*, London: Edward Arnold.

____ (ed.) (1985) *Pageantry in the Shakespearean Theater*, Athens, Ga.: University of Georgia Press.

Berry, Ralph (1972) *Shakespeare's Comedies: Explorations in Form*, Princeton: Princeton University Press.

Boose, L. (1987) "The Family in Shakespeare Studies; or – Studies in the Family of Shakespeareans; or – The Politics of Politics," *Renaissance Quarterly* XL: 707–42.

____ (1991) "Scolding Brides and Bridling Scolds: Taming the Woman's Unruly Member," *Shakespeare Quarterly* 42: 179–213.

Boswell, T., Kiser, V., and Baker, K. (1986) "Recent Developments in Marxist Theories of Ideology," *Insurgent Sociologist* 13 (4): 5–22.

Bray, A. (1988) *Homosexuality in Renaissance England*, 2nd edn, London: Gay Men's Press.

Bristol, M. (1985) *Carnival and Theater: Plebeian Culture and the Structure of Authority in Renaissance England*, London: Methuen.

Burke, P. (1978) *Popular Culture in Early Modern Europe*, London: Temple Smith.

Burt, R. (1988) " 'Tis Writ by Me': Massinger's *The Roman Actor* and the Politics of Reception in the English Renaissance Theater," *Theatre Journal* 40: 332–46.

Cahn, S. (1987) *Industry of Devotion: The Transformation of Women's Work in England, 1500–1660*, New York: Columbia University Press.

Calderwood, J. (1971) *Shakespearean Metadrama: The Argument of the Play in Titus Andronicus, Love's Labour Lost, Romeo and Juliet, A Midsummer Night's Dream, and Richard II*, Minneapolis: University of Minnesota Press.

____ (1979) *Metadrama in Shakespeare's Henriad: Richard II to Henry V*, Berkeley: University of California Press.

Candido, J. (1980) "The 'Strange Truth' of *Perkin Warbeck*," *Philological Quarterly* 59: 300–16.

Chambers, E. K. (1923) *The Elizabethan Stage*, 4 vols, Oxford: The Clarendon Press: vol. IV.

Clark, A. (1919) *Working Life of Women in the Seventeenth Century*, New York: E. P. Dutton.

Clark, P. and Soudern, D. (eds) (1988) *Migration and Society in Early Modern England*, Totowa, N. J.: Barnes and Noble.

Cohen, W. (1985) *Drama of a Nation: Public Theater in Renaissance England and Spain*, Ithaca: Cornell University Press.

—— (1987) "Political Criticism of Shakespeare," in *Shakespeare Reproduced: The Text in History and Ideology*, ed. Jean E. Howard and Marion F. O'Connor, London: Methuen: 18–46.

Conover, J. (1969) *Thomas Dekker: An Analysis of Dramatic Structure*, The Hague: Mouton.

Cook, A. (1981) *The Privileged Playgoers of Shakespeare's London, 1576–1642*, Princeton: Princeton University Press.

Cook, C. (1986) " 'The Sign and Semblance of Her Honor': Reading Gender Difference in *Much Ado About Nothing*," *Proceedings of the Modern Language Association* 101: 186–202.

Crewe, J. (1986) "The Hegemonic Theater of George Puttenham," *English Literary Renaissance* 16: 71–85.

Davis, N. (1978) "Women on Top: Symbolic Sexual Inversion and Political Disorder in Early Modern Europe," in *The Reversible World: Symbolic Inversion in Art and Society*, ed. Barbara Babcock, Ithaca, N.Y.: Cornell University Press: 147–90.

Dawson, A. (1978) *Indirections: Shakespeare and the Art of Illusion*, Toronto: University of Toronto Press.

Dekker, T. (1955) *The Dramatic Works of Thomas Dekker*, vol. II, ed. Fredson Bowers, Cambridge: Cambridge University Press.

Dennis, C. (1973) "Wit and Wisdom in *Much Ado About Nothing*," *Studies in English Literature* 13: 223–37.

Doane, M. (1982) "Film and the Masquerade: Theorizing the Female Spectator," *Screen* 23: 74–89.

Dobin, H. (1990) *Merlin's Disciples: Prophecy, Poetry and Power in Renaissance England*, Stanford: Stanford University Press.

Dollimore, J. (1984) *Radical Tragedy: Religion, Ideology and Power in the Drama of Shakespeare and His Contemporaries*, Chicago: University of Chicago Press.

—— (1987) "Subjectivity, Sexuality, and Transgression: The Jacobean Connection," *Renaissance Drama*, n.s. XVII: 53–81.

Dusinberre, J. (1975) *Shakespeare and the Nature of Women*, New York: Macmillan.

Eagleton, T. (1991) *Ideology: An Introduction*. New York: Verso.

Edwards, P. (1978) "Shakespeare and the Healing Power of Deceit," *Shakespeare Survey* 31: 115–25.

—— (1979) *Threshold of a Nation: A Study in English and Irish Drama*, New York: Cambridge University Press.

Egan, R. (1972) *Drama within Drama: Shakespeare's Sense of His Art in King Lear, The Winter's Tale, and The Tempest*, New York: Columbia University Press.

Elias, N. (1939) *The History of Manners*, vol. I of *The Civilizing Process*, 2 vols, rpt (1978) New York: Pantheon.

Erickson, P. (1987) "The Order of the Garter, the Cult of Elizabeth, and Class–Gender Tension in *The Merry Wives of Windsor*," in *Shakespeare Reproduced: The Text in History and Ideology*, ed. Jean E. Howard and Marion F. O'Connor, London: Methuen: 116–40.

Evans, G. B. (textual ed.) (1974) *The Riverside Shakespeare*, Boston: Houghton Mifflin.

Finkelpearl, P. (1986) " 'The Comedians' Liberty:' Censorship of the Jacobean Stage Reconsidered," *English Literary Renaissance* 16: 123–38.

Fisher, F. J. (1990) *London and the English Economy, 1500–1700*, ed. P. J. Corfield and N. B. Harte, London: Hambleton Press.

Fletcher, A. and Stevenson, J. (eds) (1985) *Order and Disorder in Early Modern England*, Cambridge: Cambridge University Press.

Fly, R. (1976) *Shakespeare's Mediated World*, Amherst: University of Massachusetts Press.

Foucault, M. (1979) *Discipline and Punish: The Birth of the Prison*, trans. Alan Sheridan, New York: Vintage Books.

—— (1980) *Power/Knowledge: Selected Interviews and Other Writings, 1972–77*, ed. Colin Gordon, New York: Pantheon Books.

Foxe, J. (1877) *The Acts and Monuments of John Foxe*, 4th edn, vol. III, ed. Rev. Josiah Pratt, London: The Religious Tract Society.

Fraser, R. (1970) *The War Against Poetry*, Princeton: Princeton University Press.

Gasper, J. (1990) *The Dragon and the Dove: The Plays of Thomas Dekker*, Oxford: Clarendon Press.

Goldberg, J. (1983) *James I and the Politics of Literature: Jonson, Shakespeare, Donne, and Their Contemporaries*, Baltimore: The Johns Hopkins University Press.

—— (1987) "Speculations: *Macbeth* and Source," in *Shakespeare Reproduced: The Text in History and Ideology*, ed. Jean E. Howard and Marion F. O'Connor, London: Methuen: 242–64.

—— (1992) *Sodometries*, Stanford: Stanford University Press.

Gosson, S. (1579) *The Schoole of Abuse, Conteining a Pleasaunt Invective against Poets, Pipers, Plaiers, Jesters, and such like Caterpillers of a Commonwealth*, London, STC 12097.

—— (1582) *Playes Confuted in Five Actions*, London, STC 12095.

Greenblatt, S. (1980) *Renaissance Self-Fashioning from More to Shakespeare*, Chicago: University of Chicago Press.

—— (ed.) (1982) *The Forms of Power and the Power of Forms in the Renaissance, Genre, Special Topics 7*, Norman: University of Oklahoma.

—— (1988) *Shakespearean Negotiations: The Circulation of Social Energy in Renaissance England*, Berkeley: University of California Press.

Gurr, A. (1987) *Playgoing in Shakespeare's London*, Cambridge: Cambridge University Press.

Haller, W. and M. (1941–2) "The Puritan Art of Love," *The Huntington Library Quarterly* 5: 235–72.

Hannay, M. (ed.) (1985) *Silent But For the Word: Tudor Women as Patrons, Translators, and Writers of Religious Works*, Kent, Ohio: Kent State University Press.

Haraway, D. (1988) "Situated Knowledges: The Science Question in

Feminism and the Privilege of Partial Perspective," *Feminist Studies* 14: 575–99.

Harbage, A. (1941) *Shakespeare's Audience*, New York: Columbia University Press.

Harrison, W. (1587) *The Description of England*, ed. Georges Edelen, rpt (1968) Ithaca: Cornell University Press.

Haselkorn, A., and Travitsky, B. (eds) (1990) *The Renaissance Englishwoman in Print: Counterbalancing the Canon*, Amherst: University of Massachusetts Press.

Henriques, J., Hollway, W., Urwin, K., Venn, C., and Walkerdine, V. (eds) (1984) *Changing the Subject: Psychology, Social Regulation and Subjectivity*, New York: Methuen.

Henze, R. (1971) "Deception in *Much Ado About Nothing*," *Studies in English Literature* 11: 187–201.

Heywood, T. (1874) *The Wise Woman of Hogsdon* in *The Dramatic Works of Thomas Heywood*, 6 vols, rpt (1964) London: Russell and Russell, vol. V: 275–353.

——— (1612) *An Apology for Actors*, London.

Hic Mulier or The Man-Woman and *Haec Vir or The Womanish-Man* (1620) London, rpt (1973) Ilkley, Yorkshire: Scholar Press.

Hill, C. (1964) *Society and Puritanism in Pre-Revolutionary England*, London: Secker and Warburg.

Hodgdon, B. (1991) *The End Crowns All: Closure and Contradiction in Shakespeare's History*, Princeton: Princeton University Press.

Holstun, J. (1989) "Ranting at the New Historicism," *English Literary Renaissance* 19: 189–225.

Homan, S. (1981) *When the Theater Turns to Itself: The Aesthetic Metaphor in Shakespeare*, Lewisburg, Pa.: Bucknell University Press.

Hooper, W. (1915) "The Tudor Sumptuary Laws," *English Historical Review* XXX: 433–49.

Howard, J. (1984) *Shakespeare's Art of Orchestration: Stage Technique and Audience Response*, Urbana: University of Illinois Press.

——— (1986) "The New Historicism in Renaissance Studies," *English Literary Renaissance* 16: 13–43.

——— (1988a) "Crossdressing, the Theatre, and Gender Struggle in Early Modern England," *Shakespeare Quarterly* 39: 418–40.

——— (1988b) " 'Effeminately Dolent': Gender and Legitimacy in Ford's *Perkin Warbeck*," in *John Ford: Critical Re-Visions*, ed. M. Neill, Cambridge: Cambridge University Press: 261–79.

——— (1991a) "Feminism and the Question of History: Resituating the Terms of the Debate," *Women's Studies* 19: 149–57.

——— (1991b) "Towards a Postmodern, Politically Committed Historical Practice," *Uses of History: Marxism, Postmodernism, and the Renaissance*, ed. F. Barker, P. Hulme, and M. Iversen, Manchester: Manchester University Press.

——— (1992) "Sex and Social Conflict: The Erotics of *The Roaring Girl*," in *Erotic Politics: Desire on the Renaissance Stage*, ed. Susan Zimmerman, London: Routledge: 170–90.

—— and O'Connor, M. (eds) (1987) *Shakespeare Reproduced: The Text in History and Ideology*, London: Methuen.

Hull, S. (1982) *Chaste, Silent and Obedient: English Books for Women 1475–1640*, San Marino: Huntington Library.

Huston, J. D. (1981) *Shakespeare's Comedies of Play*, New York: Columbia University Press.

Ingram, M. (1985a) "The Reform of Popular Culture? Sex and Marriage in Early Modern England," in *Popular Culture in Seventeenth-Century England*, ed. Barry Reay, New York: St Martin's Press: 129–65.

—— (1985b) "Ridings, Rough Music and Mocking Rhymes in Early Modern England," in *Popular Culture in Seventeenth-Century England*, ed. Barry Reay, New York: St Martin's Press: 166–97.

J. G. (Green?) (1615) *A Refutation of the Apology for Actors*, London.

Jackson, G. (1988) "Topical Ideology: Witches, Amazons, and Shakespeare's Joan of Arc," *English Literary Renaissance* 18: 40–65.

Jardine, L. (1983) *Still Harping on Daughters: Women and Drama in the Age of Shakespeare*, Totowa, N.J.: Barnes and Noble.

Jones, A. (1990) *The Currency of Eros: Women's Love Lyrics in Europe, 1540–1620*, Bloomington: Indiana University Press.

Jonson, B. (1963) *Bartholomew Fair*, ed. Eugene M. Waith, New Haven: Yale University Press.

—— (1966) *Epicoene or The Silent Woman*, ed. L. Beaurline, Lincoln: University of Nebraska Press.

Jorden, E. (1603) *A Briefe Discourse of a Disease called the Suffocation of the Mother*, London, STC 14790.

Kastan, D. (1986) "Proud Majesty Made a Subject: Shakespeare and the Spectacle of Rule," *Shakespeare Quarterly* 37: 459–75.

Kelly, J. (1984) "Did Women have a Renaissance?" in *Women, History, and Theory: The Essays of Joan Kelly*, Chicago: University of Chicago Press: 19–50.

Kinney, A. (1974) *Markets of Bawdrie: The Dramatic Criticism of Stephen Gosson*, Salzburg Studies in English Literature 4, Salzburg: Institut für Englische Sprache und Literatur.

Kreiger, E. (1979) "Social Relations and the Social Order in *Much Ado About Nothing*," *Shakespeare Survey* 32: 49–61.

Kuhn, A. (1985) "Sexual Disguise and Cinema," in *The Power of the Image: Essays on Representation and Sexuality*, London: Routledge: 48–73.

Lamb, M. (1990) *Gender and Authority in the Sidney Circle*, Madison: University of Wisconsin Press.

Laqueur, T. (1990) *Making Sex: Body and Gender from the Greeks to Freud*, Cambridge, Mass.: Harvard University Press.

Levine, L. (1986) "Men in Women's Clothing: Antitheatricality and Effeminization from 1579 to 1642," *Criticism* 28: 121–43.

Lodge, T. (1579–80) *A Reply to Gosson's Schoole of Abuse*, London, rpt (1973) New York: Garland Publishing Company.

MacKinnon, C. (1987) *Feminism Unmodified: Discourses on Life and Law*, Cambridge, Mass.: Harvard University Press.

McLuskie, K. (1987) "The Act, the Role, and the Actor: Boy Actresses on the Elizabethan Stage," *New Theatre Quarterly* 3: 120–30.

—— (1989) *Renaissance Dramatists*, Atlantic Highlands, N.J.: Humanities Press International.

Marcus, L. (1988) *Puzzling Shakespeare: Local Reading and Its Discontents*, Berkeley: University of California Press.

Middleton, T., and Dekker, T. (1607?) *The Roaring Girl*, ed. Andor Gomme (1976) New York: Norton.

Montrose, L. (1980a) " 'Eliza, Queene of shepheardes,' and the Pastoral of Power," *English Literary Renaissance* 10: 153–82.

—— (1980b) "The Purpose of Playing: Reflections on a Shakespearean Anthropology," *Helios* 7 (2): 51–74.

—— (1983) " 'Shaping Fantasies': Figurations of Gender and Power in Elizabethan Culture," *Representations* 2: 61–94.

—— (1986) "The Elizabethan Subject and the Spenserian Text," in *Literary Theory/Renaissance Texts*, ed. P. Parker and D. Quint, Baltimore: The Johns Hopkins University Press, 303–40.

More, Sir T. (1516) *Utopia*, trans. and ed. Robert M. Adams (1975), New York: W. W. Norton.

Moretti, F. (1982) " 'A Huge Eclipse': Tragic Form and the Deconsecration of Tragedy," in *The Forms of Power and the Power of Forms in the Renaissance*, ed. Stephen Greenblatt, *Genre, Special Topics* 7, Norman: University of Oklahoma: 7–40.

Mouffe, C. (1988) "Radical Democracy: Modern or Postmodern?" in *Universal Abandon?: The Politics of Postmodernism*, ed. A. Ross, Minneapolis: University of Minnesota Press: 31–45.

Mullaney, S. (1988a) *The Place of the Stage: License, Play, and Power in Renaissance England*, Chicago: University of Chicago Press.

—— (1988b) "The Work of Culture in an Age of Theatrical Reproduction," unpub. paper delivered at the Conference on New Languages for the Stage, University of Kansas, October.

Munday, A. (1580) *A Second and Third Blast of Retrait from Plaies and Theaters*, London, STC 21677.

Neely, C. (1988) "Constructing the Subject: Feminist Practice and the New Renaissance Discourses," *English Literary Renaissance* 18: 5–18.

Neill, M. (1976) " 'Anticke Pageantrie': The Mannerist Art of *Perkin Warbeck*," *Renaissance Drama*, n.s. 7: 117–50.

Newman, K. (1987) "Portia's Ring: Unruly Women and Structures of Exchange in *The Merchant of Venice*," *Shakespeare Quarterly* 38: 19–33.

—— (1991) *Fashioning Femininity and English Renaissance Drama*, Chicago: Chicago University Press.

Northbrooke, J. (1577) *A Treatise wherein Dicing, Dauncing, Vaine Playes or Enterluds . . . are reproved*, London, STC 18670, rpt (1974) New York: Garland Publishing.

Novy, M. (1984) *Love's Argument: Gender Relations in Shakespeare*, Chapel Hill: University of North Carolina.

Orgel, S. (1985) "Making Greatness Familiar," in *Pageantry in the Shakespearean Theater*, ed. David Bergeron, Athens, Ga.: University of Georgia Press: 19–25.

—— (1989) "Nobody's Perfect: Or Why Did the English Stage Take Boys for Women?" *The South Atlantic Quarterly* 88: 7–29.

_____ (1992) "The Subtexts of *The Roaring Girl*," in *Erotic Politics: Desire on the Renaissance Stage*, ed. Susan Zimmerman, London: Routledge: 12–26.

Park, C. (1980) "As We Like It: How a Girl can be Smart and Still Popular," in *The Woman's Part: Feminist Criticism of Shakespeare*, ed. Carol Neely *et al.*, Urbana: University of Illinois Press.

Parker, P. (1993) "Gender Ideology, Gender Change: The Case of Marie Germain," *Critical Inquiry* 19: 337–64.

Paster, G. (1985) "The Idea of London in Masque and Pageant," in *Pageantry in the Shakespearean Theater*, ed. David Bergeron, Athens, Ga.: University of Georgia Press: 48–64.

Pateman, C. (1988) *The Sexual Contract*, Stanford: Stanford University Press.

Patterson, A. (1984) *Censorship and Interpretation: The Conditions of Writing and Reading in Early Modern England*, Madison: University of Wisconsin Press.

_____ (1989) *Shakespeare and the Popular Voice*, Oxford: Basil Blackwell.

Pecheux, M. (1982) *Language, Semantics, and Ideology*, New York: St Martin's Press.

Pechter, E. (1987) "The New Historicism and Its Discontents: Politicizing Renaissance Drama," *Proceedings of the Modern Language Association* 102: 292–303.

Perkins, W. (1612) *The Workes of ... Mr. William Perkins*, vol. I, London.

Prouty, C. (1950) *The Sources of "Much Ado About Nothing,"* New Haven: Yale University Press.

Prynne, W. (1633) *Histrio-Mastix. The Players Scourge or Actors Tragedie*, London, STC 20464a.

Pye, C. (1990) *The Regal Phantasm: Shakespeare and the Politics of Spectacle*, London: Routledge.

Rackin, P. (1987) "Androgyny, Mimesis, and the Marriage of the Boy Heroine on the English Renaissance Stage," *Proceedings of the Modern Language Association* 102: 29–41.

_____ (1990) *Stages of History: Shakespeare's English Chronicles*, Ithaca: Cornell University Press.

Reay, B. (ed.) (1985) *Popular Culture in Seventeenth-Century England*, New York: St Martin's Press.

Resnick, S., and Wolff, R. (1982) "Marxist Epistemology: The Critique of Economic Determinism," *Social Text* 2 (3): 31–72.

Ribner, I. (1965) *The English History Play in the Age of Shakespeare*, rev. edn, New York: Barnes and Noble.

Righter, A. (1962) *Shakespeare and the Idea of the Play*, London: Chatto and Windus.

Ringler, W. (1942) *Stephen Gosson: A Bibliographical and Critical Study*, Princeton: Princeton University Press.

Rose, M. (1972) *Shakespearean Design*, Cambridge: The Belknap Press of Harvard University Press.

Rose, M. B. (ed.) (1986) *Women in the Middle Ages and the Renaissance: Literary and Historical Perspectives*, Syracuse: Syracuse University Press.

—— (1988) *The Expense of Spirit: Love and Sexuality in English Renaissance Drama*, Ithaca: Cornell University Press.

Ross, A. (ed.) (1988) *Universal Abandon?: The Politics of Postmodernism*, Minneapolis: University of Minnesota Press.

Rossiter, A. (1961) *Angel with Horns and Other Shakespeare Lectures*, ed. Graham Storey, London: Longmans.

Rozett, M. (1984) *The Doctrine of Election and the Emergence of Elizabethan Tragedy*, Princeton: Princeton University Press.

Rubin, G. (1975) "The Traffic in Women: Notes on the 'Political Economy' of Sex," in *Toward an Anthropology of Women*, ed. Rayna R. Reiter, New York: Monthly Review Press: 157–210.

—— (1984) "Thinking Sex: Notes for a Radical Theory of the Politics of Sexuality," in *Pleasure and Danger: Exploring Female Sexuality*, ed. Carole S. Vance, New York: Routledge: 267–319.

Schochet, G. (1975) *Patriarchalism in Political Thought: The Authoritarian Family and Political Speculation and Attitudes, Especially in Seventeenth-Century England*, Oxford: Basil Blackwell.

Scot, R. (1584) *The Discoverie of Witchcraft*, ed. Brinsley Nicholson (1886) London: Elliot Stack.

Sermons or Homilies Appointed to be Read in Churches in the Time of Queene Elizabeth Of Famous Memory, 4th edn (1816), Oxford: Clarendon Press.

Sharp, B. (1980) *In Contempt of All Authority: Rural Artisans and Riot in the West of England 1586–1660*, Berkeley: University of California Press.

Shepherd, S. (1981) *Amazons and Warrior Women: Varieties of Feminism in Seventeenth-Century Drama*, Brighton: Harvester Press.

Sidney, Sir P. (1595) *An Apology for Poetry or The Defence of Poesy*, ed. Geoffrey Shepherd (1965), New York: Barnes and Noble.

Smith, B. (1991) *Homosexual Desire in Shakespeare's England: A Cultural Poetics*, Chicago: University of Chicago Press.

Sorge, T. (1987) "The Failure of Orthodoxy in *Coriolanus*," in *Shakespeare Reproduced: The Text in History and Ideology*, ed. Jean E. Howard and Marion F. O'Connor, London: Methuen: 225–41.

Stallybrass, P. (1986) "Patriarchal Territories: The Body Enclosed," in *Rewriting the Renaissance: The Discourses of Sexual Difference in Early Modern England*, ed. M. Ferguson, M. Quilligan, and N. Vickers, Chicago: University of Chicago Press: 123–42.

Staves, S. (1979) *Players' Scepters: Fictions of Authority in the Restoration*, Lincoln: University of Nebraska Press.

Stone, L. (1965) *The Crisis of the Aristocracy, 1558–1641*, Oxford: Clarendon Press.

—— (1966) "Social Mobility in England, 1500–1700," *Past and Present* 33: 16–55.

—— (1972) *The Causes of the English Revolution, 1529–1642*, London: Routledge and Kegan Paul.

—— (1977) *The Family, Sex and Marriage in England 1500–1800*, New York: Harper and Row.

Stubbes, P. (1583) *The Anatomie of Abuses*, London, STC 23376.

171

Swetnam, J. (1615) *The Araignment of Lewde, idle, froward and unconstant women: Or the vanitie of them, choose you whether*, London, STC 23533.

Therborn, G. (1980) *The Ideology of Power and the Power of Ideology*, London: Verso.

Thirsk, J. (1978) *Economic Policy and Projects: The Development of a Consumer Society in Early Modern England*, Oxford: Clarendon Press.

Thomas, K. (1971) *Religion and the Decline of Magic*, New York: Charles Scribner's Sons.

Tilney, E. (1587) *A Briefe and pleasant discourse of duties in Mariage called the Flower of Friendship*, London.

Traub, V. (1992) *Desire and Anxiety: Circulations of Sexuality in Shakespearean Drama*, London: Routledge.

Travitsky, B. (1981) *The Paradise of Women: Writings by Englishwomen of the Renaissance*, Westport, Conn.: Greenwood Press.

Tuke, T. (1616) *A Treatise Against Painting and Tincturing of Men and Women*, London, STC 24316.

Underdown, D. (1985) "The Taming of the Scold: The Enforcement of Patriarchal Authority in Early Modern England," in *Order and Disorder in Early Modern England*, ed. Anthony Fletcher and John Stevenson, Cambridge: Cambridge University Press: 116–36.

―― (1987) *Revel, Riot, and Rebellion: Popular Politics and Culture in England 1603–1660*, New York: Oxford University Press.

Venuti, L. (1989) *Our Halcyon Dayes: English Prerevolutionary Texts and Postmodern Culture*, Madison: University of Wisconsin Press.

Waller, M. (1987) "Academic Tootsie: The Denial of Difference and the Difference It Makes," *Diacritics* 17: 2–20.

Watson, D. (1990) *Shakespeare's Early History Plays: Politics at Play on the English Stage*, London: Macmillan.

Wayne, D. (1987) "Power, Politics, and the Shakespearean Text: Recent Criticism in England and the United States," in *Shakespeare Reproduced: The Text in History and Ideology*, ed. Jean E. Howard and Marion F. O'Connor, London: Methuen: 47–67.

Weimann, R. (1978) *Shakespeare and the Popular Tradition in the Theater: Studies in the Social Dimension of Dramatic Form and Function*, ed. R. Schwartz, Baltimore: The Johns Hopkins University Press.

―― (1987) "Towards a Literary Theory of Ideology: Mimesis, Representation Authority," in *Shakespeare Reproduced: The Text in History and Ideology*, ed. Jean E. Howard and Marion F. O'Connor, London: Methuen: 265–72.

Whigham, F. (1984) *Ambition and Privilege: The Social Tropes of Elizabethan Courtesy Theory*, Berkeley: University of California Press.

Wilson, K. (ed.) (1987) *Women Writers of the Renaissance and Reformation*, Athens, Ga.: University of Georgia Press.

Winny, J. (1968) *The Player King: A Theme of Shakespeare's Histories*, London: Chatto and Windus.

Woodbridge, Linda (1984) *Women and the English Renaissance: Literature and the Nature of Womankind, 1540–1620*, Urbana: University of Illinois Press.

Wright, L. (1935) *Middle-Class Culture in Elizabethan England*, Chapel Hill: University of North Carolina.

Wrightson, K. (1982) *English Society, 1580–1680*, New Brunswick: Rutgers University Press.

Yates, F. (1975) *Astraea: The Imperial Theme in the Sixteenth Century*, London: Routledge and Kegan Paul.

Zimmerman, Susan (ed.) (1992) *Erotic Politics: Desire on the Renaissance Stage*, London: Routledge.

Zitner, S. (1958) "Gosson, Ovid, and the Elizabethan Audience," *Shakespeare Quarterly* 9: 206–8.

INDEX

INDEX

Montrose, L. 10, 154n4, 156n5, 156n6
morality plays 142
Moretti, F. 156n5
Morocco (*The Merchant of Venice*) 117
Morose (*Epicoene*) 107, 108, 109
Mortimer 137, 148, 149
Mouffe, C. 158n5
Much Ado About Nothing (Shakespeare) 15–16, 46, 49, 57–72, 84, 86, 157n5
Mullaney, S. 12, 31, 79, 82–3, 155n6
Munday, A. 156n7

Neely, C. 12
new historicism 8, 11, 12, 45, 82, 158n6
Newman, K. 32, 102, 156n6, 161–2n15
Northbrooke, J. 6, 23–31, 45, 93, 139; social order 35; vagrants 36, 80; on women 79, 80, 91
Novy, M. 118
Nussbaum, H. 78, 158n2

Olivia 112, 113, 114–15, 116, 120
Orgel, S. 11, 97, 161n12
Orlando (*As You Like It*) 118, 119, 120, 129
Orsino 113, 114, 115, 116
Otter, Mrs. 106, 108, 109
Otter, T. 106, 107, 108
Ovid 75, 158n1

painting *see* women; comsetics
Papists 1, 2, 3
Park, C. 160n2
Parker, P. 160n5
Paster, G. 156n9
Pateman, C. 161n11
patriarchy 77, 78, 79, 92, 94, 100, 161n11; authority 104, 108, 116–17, 162n15; ideology 13, 121; marriage 17, 89, 91, 116, 125, 126, 127, 128, 149; *The Merchant of Venice* 117–18; *Much Ado About Nothing* 68–9;

oppression 20; position of women 119; power 3, 91, 114, 161n9
patriotism 48, 59, 56, 157n3
Patterson, A. 137, 155n7
Pecheux, M. 158n5
Pechter, E. 155n8
Pedro, Don 57, 59, 61–71, 86
Perkin Warbeck (Ford) 17
Perkins, W. 155–6n4
Petruchio 107
Peter (apprentice to Horner) *see* Thump, P.
Philips, K. 110
Phoebe 120
Pico *see* Mirandola, Pico della
Pistol 63
Plaine-dealing 51, 54, 55–6
Platter, T. 104
Playes Confuted in Five Actions (Gosson) 40
playgoing 73–4, 158n1; apparel 75; ideology of 73–80, 83–4, 90–2; material practices 83; politics of 80; variable impact 76; women 73, 76, 77, 80, 84, 90, 91, 92, 109
political criticism 19–20, 21, 155n8, 155n9
Pompey (*Measure for Measure*) 64
Portia 116–17, 118, 119, 128, 161–2n15
priests 1, 6, 37–8, 51–2, 100; apparel 160n7
prostitution 95, 96, 100
Protestants 3, 28, 41, 108, 136, 157n3, 157n4; marriage 104; *The Whore of Babylon* 51, 52, 53, 54, 56
Prouty, C. 59, 62
Prynne, W. 6, 93
public theater 3, 4, 10, 12–18, 58, 73–80, 82, 152–3; antitheatrical tracts 22, 23, 26, 42, 43; audience 10, 13, 14, 30, 34, 160n2; idleness 25; impact on social groups 16; political implications 73, 84; role in ideological production 3, 4,

181